Son, You Turn
A Good Phrase

by Stockton Todd Holden

Printed in the United States of America
First Printing, 2015

ISBN 978-0-9860911-0-0

Cairn of Quartz Publishing
315 East Broadway
Bel Air, MD 21014

Book design, production, and editing by Patrick M. Wallis

Cover Photograph of the author's father, Gwynne LeRoy Holden, by the author's son, Samuel Gwynne Holden.

The author would like to thank the Ace Team, who keep the flame burning; the recently departed Lady Frisco, who is buried next to Koda and where Sammy's ashes are spread; and my vigilant companions Lord Nelson aka The Dude, and of course Lord Chesterfield aka Chesternutz... stalwart companions, loyal and loving.

There are others of course, my wonderful daughter, Mina, her loving family, Todd, Grayson, Silas and Scarlett...I'm a lucky guy...there are many others to thank and many who helped bring this book to fruition. You will find them all within the pages of this book. True friends.

Front cover photo by Sam Holden

1969-2014

Self Portrait of Sam Holden, Berlin Wall, 2008

"Let me know if you need this tuned up."

Note From The Editor

Been through hell and back getting this book planted and this time it just might take root. On the good days, dealing with Todd is about the closest thing to a good feeling as one can get. On the bad days, well, let's just say there weren't many of them. 'So far, so good' was the code of the road and the pleasure has been all mine.

Indeed, music has been a large part of the friendship, along with the sharing of friends and family and some unadulterated adventures better left in the scrapbook.

Yes, the rewards are other worldly and most gratifying. These are stories that transcend time and chronology, and for the most part don't need a lot of reference to bring across a point...a point well made with only a few short pages...others have tried, few have come close.

That's what makes it precious. Of course, one writes because one has to...it's in the blood, so to speak. Writing ties the common man with the elite, the politician with the romantic, and the revolutionary with the patriot.

Writing gives voice to those who cannot express themselves, explains the mundane as well as the complicated, delivers perspective where a flat line exists, expresses hope in the midst of despair, and gives love in the heart where nothing resides. All of that and infinitely more. As each individual is distinct, through the ages, so too are the ways to pen thoughts, express the dreams and desires, and affect the mind just enough to keep it going.

The stories on the following pages are short and to the point...written by a man who can define character in a total stranger, slow down the moment to consider a simple truth, and bend time to offer a keen perspective on the notions described here on these pages.

Herein are stories of truth, both in the telling and what is told. They are words...they will not rust with time or be captured by it. They come from a man who delivers a slice of time with precision and a cool glass of story telling sure to quench your thirst.

Have a seat and read from cover to cover. Or better yet, pick it up anywhere in between and be content with where you land. It's a good read. Enjoy!

Wolf Wallis

Author's Foreword

My heroes were men and women like Wilson Ford, Winfield Mitchell, Dale Coale, Charley Richardson, Mary Bristow, Addie Holden, Carl Dean Todd, Lacy Francis, Grayson Hopkins, Celie Wisner...names that mean nothing to most, a ton to me.

These were the folks I looked up to for the way they ran their lives, did their work, shared their love and told their stories. Whether they knew it at the time or not, they were shaping me and molding me to be the person I am today.

Somewhere along the way, the torch was passed, because now I'm making my own stories and affecting the lives of those who I've befriended. It's history repeating itself, again and again. We get, we give, we share, we live our lives the best we can and along the way folks drift in and out of that life. Ultimately, we are in the position of being more relevant to others just because we've lived this long.

The passing of the day into night and then morning comes and rebuilds us, makes us whole again for another round of life. The touchstones we build our lives on are varied and confusing at times, but also we learn from this that there are no secrets to the game of life. It's all out there in front of us if we are wise enough to see the values of our mentors and embrace the good, pass on the values to others we come to share destiny with.

So many converging influences have brought me to this place, standing tall and contemplating the next steps to take. There has been no plan, no road map, no strategy...just me looking at lots of scribble about things I've seen and heard and figuring maybe a tale could be told that would explain what in my mind I saw as noteworthy.

So many books have registered with me long after reading them...guides, if you will, of a path that's been shared and insights for the taking. This collection is a guide as well, paths I've made and ones I've come across.

Honestly, I never took any of this seriously and believed life would be fine if a book never came to be. My editor and collaborator, Pat 'Wolf' Wallis started collecting articles. He did this with vengeance and vigilance and vision. Wolf put the book together and handed it to me for editing.

Yes, here I was editing my own work, something the laziness in me was appalled by. I didn't want to re-read my stuff; after all, it had been edited, submitted, published and saved in the files. I'm happy just being a scribbler. Hell, half of it I don't remember writing, these were glimpses of my viewfinder on the passing scene. Events significant to me and perhaps fun to write... never did I write to please anyone other than myself, the writing was the rush.

Honestly, the reason I write is purely selfish.

Then, one of those converging influences came into play...no plan, no road map, and no strategy.

The book was in my hands and now it was my turn to get to work. It was a bitch, but I devised a plan of attack that involved Katy Dallam's scrumptious Maryland crab soup and a quiet corner of her eatery, after the lunch hour rush. It was the perfect atmosphere for total concentration and absorption for the task at hand, to read and correct mistakes before a publisher puts out something that might be an embarrassment to everyone.

So thanks Katy for letting me while away hours at your table.

Ironically most of the people mentioned in the first paragraph were not close to the man on the cover of this book...my dad. You see, he didn't suffer most of my pals, he observed them with a watchful eye and moved on. Yet when I wrote, relating to their influence, he would sometimes, not all the time, utter those words that drove my spirit...'Son, you turn a good phrase'...that's been the icing on this cake of life.

You will be introduced to a few of the dear people I have known through the years, but by no means all. These are all your stories now. Perhaps you too have written for the sheer joy of writing and letting your thoughts and visions land on paper to be seen by others and hopefully enjoyed. The journey continues....

Prologue

When I was young, I spent a lot of time with my eyes wide open and my ears to the wind. There was always someone to learn from...an adventure to be had. Life on the farm was life in the big city to me and the experiences I had I wouldn't trade for the world.

Those encounters, those adventures with friends or total strangers, at the post office or in the middle of nowhere, molded me into the man I am today. Since the time I can remember, I've had the urge to create. For a long time, the bread and butter was photography, working at *The Aegis*, at one time the biggest and best weekly newspaper in Harford County, and then with my own photography studio. Writing was always part of the urge, although I didn't realize for a long time what I was doing.

I always kept a journal, a diary of events in my life. I knew what I was putting to paper was decently good material, but it wasn't until I closed the studio in 2001 that I began writing in earnest and knowing I had something going.

A lot of folks you meet on these pages are family and friends and people I know. Many of them have ties to Rustica and visit frequently. Rustica is the name of the peaceful preserve in which I live. I lived there with my wife, Ann, and we raised two beautiful children, Sam and Mina. As I write this introduction, Sam has recently

left this earth in bodily form, but still keeps watch over Rustica. With my wife passed as well, my darling Mina and I are the strongholds of the Holdens on this land our family has farmed on since 1953.

These stories are a collection of columns I've written over the years that have been published in various newspapers, notably *The Delta Star*, a newspaper of the small town of Delta where a lot of my history lies. You will read of snapshots of people I've met, dealings with nature and animals, and conversations and encounters with locals of all types. My pen is not primed with the ink of the rich and prominent. Far from it, my interest follows the men and women who have so much to offer and so little recognition along the way. That is the meat for my ink.

I've had the pleasure of a full life with many twists and turns and these pages share that adventure. These are the scribbles and observations of one with his eyes wide open and his ears to the wind and his heart filled with anticipation for the stranger with a song to sing, a tale to tell or a helping hand.

STH

The Fox Always Wins

The Walden Experiment continues here at Rustica, albeit with some minor fine tuning. To wit: still have to pull out poison ivy from evergreens, flower beds and borders. Still need to cut down wild locust trees growing up through spruce, pine and fir, as well as wild grape and bittersweet. For the most part, though, the habitat is pro-wildlife, easy to tend to and suited for someone like me.

You see, I tend to be lazy but I do take seriously the calling I have as caretaker of this pristine piece of land. I learn more as each season changes and am always in awe of the beauty of the wild things that grow and crawl and survive here on Rustica.

There are five peafowl here and Elvis presides as the fully adorned cock of the ranch. He is casting seeds of life to two mature peahens and they are brooding eggs. Not always in the most secretive of places though. One nest is out in the open near a Norway spruce and any day now they will hatch out. There are only two eggs under her and they will be checked twice a day so once they hatch, the peeps can then be moved into the coop with the hen. It's about the only way to keep fresh fry from foxes, coons or opossums.

Soybeans are planted this year, and the low, bushy cover affords foxes the chance to visit close by and see what's on the menu.

No matter how many banties are here, the foxes always win out. It's just a matter of time for the chickens. Even the best and most wary of them will be undone and done in by the red fox, the most adaptive carnivore in North America.

The debate is to continue with birds like banties and peafowl as long as there are foxes living here as well. Punky Probst who must have well over 200 peafowl on her farm just north of Fountain Green, told me recently the trapper who works her place took 59 last year, along with a field rat, nine coons and a couple of opossums.

"Fifty Nine!! I thought I had it bad here with the one or two I've seen traveling the same paths. She has over two hundred peafowl and five dozen foxes, and for now the foxes are losing, thanks to man's traps. Well, I guess that's okay because the foxes will continue their pursuit and without the trapper they will win. So this victory for Punky is only temporary and she knows it.

Now the eggs will hatch here, and to live the fledglings must be caught within twenty-four hours of hatching and put up where it's safe. So, we help Mother Nature out a bit and enjoy the little ones, knowing full well they are on borrowed time, as are the rest of us. Except the foxes. They will always win. And the Walden Experiment continues.

========= 30 =========

A New Puppy

I read the Star each week, all of it, especially the classifieds, obits and front page...and oh yeah, The Column. This one caught my eye

> "CUTE JACK RUSSELL pups, Mother good farm dog. Males $175, females $200. Shots and Wormed. Daniel Lapp, 301 Tyson Road, Fawn Grove, PA. 17321."

No phone number, eh? but a zip code...hmmm? Intriguing information. A brief discussion with my 'significant other'...Frisco, and we decided to head north to try to find this Lapp chap.

At the intersection in Fawn Grove, a lady gave me sketchy directions, but I did manage to find Maple Farm, or some such name, and the fellow there suggested that with the name of Daniel Lapp, it had to be an Amish man. That answers the telephone question.

With the zip code, I guess mail would be the way to get directions but the gentleman gave me good ones... turn on Bridgton, go to the second lane, that would be Tyson, and look for the name on a mailbox.

Well, the road curves and a little jog goes off to the right, sure enough, with all that black and white laundry hanging on the long line across the lawn to a pole, this

must be the place. Frisco was alert too, thinking 'we finally found this place.'

Long lane, neat as a pin...laundry blowing in the wind so I drive slowly down the dusty lane and turn around behind the barns...figuring I'd give whoever lived there time to see me and come out. Down near Bel Air that same move usually allows the property owner to shut all the windows and lock all the doors...either that or load up and come out with a gun.

After all, Frisco and I thought, this was supposedly an Amish man, so we kept recalling 'the gentle people'...then, out the door comes a man, friendly and unassuming.

I ask if he's the one who's got the pups. "Yes, I do," he replies. Meanwhile Frisco has jumped out, sniffed out Daniel Lapp and proceeds to eliminate on the lawn. Which I didn't see, but Lapp did.

"Oh that's alright," Daniel says, "It all goes back into the ground."...Well, thanks for allowing that minor infraction Daniel. Already, I'm at ease in his company and have a good feeling about this.

We proceed to the dairy barn and the litter of Jack Russells...I think there's 8 of them. This is where much thought must be given, whenever selecting a puppy. I clap my hands loudly, a few cringe, others do not...these are the ones I'm interested in, they're not skittish, they are unthwarted in their curiosity, just as I am of them.

Next, they try to get out of the stall to check me and Frisco out. One makes it over the two by six plank and turns out to be beautifully marked.

We proceed out to the lawn near the spot where Frisco left her calling card...I go there purposely to allow the pup to sniff the ground. Sure enough, he drops and tinkles, another good sign.

In the training here at Rustica, Frisco has a few places around the tractor shed to do her thing, so when the grandkids come up or any pals are tossing the Frisbee with Frisco, they don't step in anything. It's really easy to train a dog where to go, and this little fella seems to have the moxey to learn the ways of good behavior.

Dude feeling right at home. Photo by Todd Holden.

I didn't know whether or not it was a male, which it was, and that suited me because immediately there was a connection with the pup. Usually there is some trepidation when I spend money on anything...like withdrawal pains or fear of not doing the right thing. But this seemed so right and we settled up on the pup.

Years ago I raised Jack Russells and enjoyed them to no end. So here I have a pal for Frisco and me, who will add to the spirit of peace and fun here at home.

On the way home from Lapp's, the pup snuggled up under a pillow in the back of the Expedition and fell asleep.

I stopped near Muddy Creek and let both dogs out, in a hayfield, with plenty of room. Frisco knows why I stop often when we travel, and sure enough the little fella did too. Matter of fact it was a 'triple pit stop' if you know what I mean. Bonding is important and I'm one to do my part.

So far, so good. Haven't come up with a name yet... just hasn't hit me...takes time to name a dog or any pet for that matter. Puppy will do for now.

He and Frisco get along great, but man, are his teeth sharp....brings back fond memories of raising dogs so many years ago. One thing for sure, Daniel Lapp has some good pups and they are smart and gentle.

Some folks don't care for Jack Russells, saying they are mean, or hard headed...whatever...usually it's the owners who are mean or hard headed, not the pups. The owner is the master but it's a different kind of relationship. You've got to be a good friend too.

Frisco and Dude, not long after Dude became part of the family.
Photo by Todd Holden.

Since the pups were raised in Lapp's barn, mine likes
to lounge on a big puppy bed in the garage and has
adjusted well.

Main thing is Frisco and he have become pals in less
than a week. The vet checked him out a couple days
after he arrived here. So we're on our way with this
addition for friendship and love.

I haven't told the children yet...because I might just
get a lecture and admonishment asking why I need a
puppy to take care of. Well, no one said anything about
'needing anything'...it's just a matter of appreciation and
growth...for me, Frisco and the pup. Least ways, that's
the way I look at it.

========= 30 =========

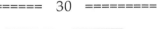

When Do You Want
To Come Home?

Looks like the ruby-throated hummingbirds have headed south a little early this year. It was a good year for them here at my place. I counted at least three families and traced their flight paths to determine where the nests were.

I've only found one little, lichen-laced nest here and that was several years ago. A little larger than a golf ball cut in half.

I miss the hummers appearing in regularity at the sole feeder outside my den window. The days seem incomplete without them. We are spoiled so easily... maybe that's why so much of the world today hates us. Because we enjoy life and the simple pleasures it gives and some folks just think that's greedy and uncalled for.

On TV yesterday was a chorus and orchestra in Vienna. A glorious feast of symphony music. A large audience in a huge soccer stadium. I couldn't understand the language, but there were subtitles to help the viewer along. The program was part of a 'fund raising' effort for Maryland Public TV

What struck me was everyone was modestly dressed, regular working class people. Europeans one and all. They sang along together when the maestro beckoned them to join in. They were happy people enjoying ageless music performed by an eclectic group of men and women and children.

For a moment I wondered why can't that happen here in our country? Are we so unfortunate that the smiles and innocence are gone forever from our hearts here? Why did it strike me the way it did? What is so wrong with innocence today?

There's innocence and naiveté...and they are not to be confused. We've all been made fun of for being 'out of it' or naïve when we've missed the point or not laughed on cue or not 'got' a painting or a poem or an idea. And that's okay with me, because there are times I like the innocence of being in the dark.

It's a great place to be sometimes. A little girl I know is autistic and she comes to me when I beckon her to my arms. She loves to hug me and look in my eyes. She speaks only rarely but laughs a lot and in her way communicates with love and touch and breath and eyes and beauty.

There is no hesitation in her innocence. There shouldn't be any in love, respect, or in the offer of help or being helped by another person.

The television is filled with anger from folks living in Louisiana and Mississippi, and friends there have told me the story not shown on the television and that's a sad fact with the media today. If you are to learn the truth

in any event, you need to know the whole story. Not the half but the whole.

A friend tells you the truth, regardless of political differences or race or age. We need to be honest with each other and take the time to be sure the facts are straight and then, and only then, decide how we feel.

Heck, it doesn't even take that long. We hear and feel at the same time, don't we?

Like the ruby-throats know when the time to leave has come, we too should know the time to stop the listening to one-sided stories and take the time to know when to leave the conversation because it's not good for our health to continue to be lied to.

The birds don't know more than us, they just know how to go with their inner spirit.

========= 30 =========

The Haves and Have Nots

This year the ruby-throated hummingbird was either abundant or scarce, and it mattered little whether or not you put the right mixture out, or how many feeders you had. A buddy of mine in West Virginia, Herbie McComsey, said he was using about a half gallon of sugar water a week for his hummers. Spikey "Pooh" Updegrove said he hardly had any at his place in Tudor Manor, Bel Air.

This is what is fascinating about birding, you never know what the year will bring, or what birds will be abundant and which ones will be in short supply.

"I didn't get any till August 15th, probably the ones starting to head south, traveling 1,000's of miles. If they had been nesting here I would have had more earlier," Updegrove said. The hummingbirds here at Rustica were nesting, three pair of them, each pair in a different direction when they flew from the lone feeder I have outside the den window.

This was the most prolific year for hummers here, no doubt about it. It's probably due to the fact my buddy Keith Holbrook and I installed three honeybee hives in the pasture early in the spring. We had to feed the new colonies a mix of equal parts water and sugar, and sometimes a little of the mixture was left over and that went to the hummingbird feeder.

It was really a 'high-octane' mixture and they loved it. I don't like to feed too much sugar, just because I don't think it's good for the birds, just like any high sugar foods aren't good for us...maybe that's wrong thinking, comparing us to birds, but that's how I think, and it's not likely to change.

The words of Wilson Ford always ring true when it comes to wildlife... "you have to think like a hummingbird to know what to do for a hummingbird." ...or any other creature of nature for that matter.

Other birds that seemed extra plentiful this year were red-breasted nuthatches and white-breasted as well. Lots of downy woodpeckers too, and the family of Pileated's nested farther down the wood line this year. The old snag they were in two years ago blew over during the big rains we had late in the spring, so they knew better by not using it this year.

Great blue herons have done well too, taking care of business along the edge of the pond and around the lily pads. Missing in action this year are box turtles and black snakes. Haven't seen but one box turtle all season here, and thankfully, not many road kills. The ray of hope though was two baby black rat snakes crawling along the carport a couple weeks ago. Somewhere they hatched out, nearby, maybe in the tractor shed. Haven't seen any adults and no sheds from them either.

STH

Anytime young are around it's a good sign, so maybe next year will bring more. The box turtles might have had a bad time with all the heavy rains we had early on this year, not sure if that affects them or not. The fields are full of soy beans, so any critters that are moving about, like red fox, are out of sight now.

White-tail deer are doing great, two herds of them, and a couple big bucks. Most folks aren't fond of white tails, because of their liking shrubbery and other garden varieties. My daughter, Mina, can't keep anything around her yard over in Hunt Valley, and they've tried everything to deter the deer. Here, they stick to the soy beans or corn when it's the crop John Magness plants, so I have no complaints in that department.

All in all the weather this year was like a roller coaster, as I'm sure it was with most of the county and southern Pennsylvania. The migration is beginning, and less and less hummers will be at the feeder, soon they will be heading to South America.

The feeder is still half full, and when it's gone, and there's not a lot of action, I'll take it down, clean it up and put it away till next year. You might want to do the same. Nothing worse than leaving a feeder outside in the winter, empty...seems to show a disregard to nature and the season.

========= 30 =========

Decisive Moments

B ear with me on this one, valued readers. A bit of nostalgia overcame me this morning and it had to be written...it has to do with 'letting go' and 'holding on to stuff' that means little to anyone else but you. Something you've kept, for some good reason long forgotten, and there comes a time when you have to ask yourself why.

That said, getting to the point is a lesson learned from a neighbor just a few minutes ago. Back in 1966, I began creating photographs, first for newspapers and then for folks who liked my work. Over 35 years of photography brought me a lot of satisfaction and self expression, and helped pay a lot of bills. When I closed the studio in 2002 there were over 65,000 negatives to go through, to be saved, or just tossed and burned. A little bit of me went into each one of those 65,000 or so negatives and just to chuck them felt awkward.

There were many shots of weddings and the photographs that went straight to paying bills. Many portraits had a history or a story to them that transcended the moment they were taken and became part of some larger context. There were also many of a different bend, closer to the celebration of the craft of photography and the capturing of local flavor that have frozen time and tell their own story.

Many of the negatives and photographs were turned over by request to the Historical Society of Harford County where they 'semi-created' a legacy to my craft, an archive as it were. More work, more sifting through to find out what to let go of and what to hold onto. Handing over the boxes was richly rewarding, though, to know some of my stuff was good enough to hold onto in a repository for the ages.

Lots of portraits were of notable folks, farmers, businessmen and women, educators, and just regular people who cared about other people. No ego involved, just a great sense of pride that my work had longevity beyond that simple click of the lens.

O.K., that done, there were still 50,000 or so more negatives to cull through, mostly toss away. There were lots of them that were just strangers to me and it wasn't too hard to part with now. Sounds cold, but 50,000 faces staring back at you through a negative or a photograph can be an overwhelming experience.

When I came across a portrait made, say in the 70s or 80s of someone still in the area, I just couldn't toss it, so I would call or see the person, and offer them the negatives, previews or prints...no charge of course. Most were glad to reminisce and took the offer. Just as rewarding as my contribution to the Historical Society, maybe even more, was the returning, as it were, of these captured moments in time to their original subjects. Still, much of what I've gone through has been tossed, because folks are gone, literally or figuratively.

Until this morning, when I came across a family portrait of three brothers, two of them with their wives, and one, who was single then and is married now and a neighbor of mine. So I called him and mentioned the 'file' and asked if he wanted it.

"No, Todd...you can just throw it away," he said. It was fine with me, and that was it. I didn't ask him why he didn't want the portrait and at first it seemed odd that he wouldn't even be interested in looking at it. Then the lesson was learned...sometimes folks just want to forget what I captured in time. At the time it was good work, the subjects were happy, satisfied and made big orders. But for me, it was 'then'...for them, it was 'then' as well...and that was good.

Things change over the years, photographs don't... images remain the same, locked in time. Decades pass along, we live on, the photographs do also...better than our memories most times, eh?

Families 'wax and wane' and drift apart over issues that aren't resolved, or feelings that are hurt. Perhaps such was the case this morning, and without getting into it, suffice to say it doesn't really matter...just a memory that my neighbor didn't care to revisit. Taking a last look at the portrait I was satisfied it was a good one, and for what it was it did the job. From my recollection and what I know about my neighbor, it captured that frozen moment in time before the waxing and waning began. Now its time is past and the story is no longer mine.

STH

I'm still going through the final two cardboard boxes of 'family history'...when a familiar face comes up again, depending on how easy it is to contact the person, I may offer it, if they want it. If they don't, I understand.

Years ago I gave a friend a framed portrait of one of his best pals who happens to be an artist of some renown. Later on when I visited his home on Main street in Delta I noticed the portrait was nowhere to be found... and I asked about it.

"Why would I want to hang a portrait of him?" was the reply...then I was told it was in the garage. Wow! Talk about a 'reality check'...so, it's not what I think is valuable and worth saving...not at all. When it comes to commissioned work that I did it's the work I've done from the heart, for me, that matters.

Daily it seems, someone I run into when I'm out and about or on Facebook will comment they still have the album I shot, or the portrait is still on their wall, 'proudly displayed' or simply, "Todd, you were the best. We're glad we chose you."

The portraits created were from the heart too, but for those who they were done for hearts may change. And that's okay. The lesson is to not take one's self too seriously, and to have compassion for those whose family members, like some of mine, have withered and fallen from the vine. All still, precious mem'ries.

========= 30 =========

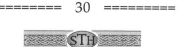

The Glow In The Dark, Blessed Virgin Mary Holy Water Font

There were only two Presbyterians in the 7th grade at St. Margaret School and I was one of them. The other was Johnny Clark, who, following 'graduation' in 1953 went on to some school for the delinquent rich in southern Maryland. Me...I proudly graduated St. Margaret and went on to public high school in my hometown of Bel Air.

We had 'recess' at St. Margaret twice a day, not including lunch time, when I walked home usually to have lunch with my mom and my brother. A Catholic school in a rural town in Maryland in the early 50s was a good place for learning. I learned a lot and there was stern discipline to back it up.

First thing after we gathered in the classroom and prayed was catechism and even though I did not have to take it, I had to listen, or on occasion, was sent to the First National Bank six or so blocks from the school with the collection funds from church services and bingo.

In that little cigar box that I so carefully guarded but never once looked inside of...me the little Presbyterian, near-sighted, buck-teeth, kinda nerdy fella...carrying money to the bank for Father Joseph McCourt and the School Sisters of Notre Dame. For me, it was a big deal.

It came to pass the archdiocese sponsored a writing contest for our school. Amazingly, I won first prize even though I can't quite recall what I wrote about. But I won. I was so proud and happy when Sister Hillaire read my name along with the runners-up.

First prize was a glow in the dark, Blessed Virgin Mary holy water font, suitable for mounting on the wall. It was the Blessed Mother with a blue veil and open arms outstretched to the little pool where holy water was used for the dipping of fingers.

"Let's see it," my Dad said, and I presented the Blessed Mother at the dinner table. My mother laughed and then got real serious when Dad asked what we should do with it. Excitedly, I answered, "Put it up, please, in the hallway at the front door, then everyone can have holy water when they come in...please Dad, please."

And so it was done. With care not to shatter the plastic hanger on the back, Dad mounted the Blessed Mother on the wallpapered wall just inside the front door of our home on Hickory avenue, a mere block from the St. Margaret Convent, school and church.

"Well son, if it's gonna be done, it's gonna be done right...get some holy water and we'll fill it," Dad ordered. He gave me a clear empty bottle of some sort and off I went to meet with Father McCourt for the 'fill up'...We went to the sacristy and he dipped the clear glass bottle into the sacred water and I took it home and Dad filled the font with it.

I think I was the only one who used it, every time I used the front door, which wasn't that often. When Dad had a poker game with his pals, some of them used it when they came and when they left. They were 'grown up Catholics' and Dad put a stop to it before the poker games. Something about an 'unfair advantage.'

Soon the water was all gone and I had to get more. When I asked Father McCourt if we could have some more holy water he nodded in agreement and suggested this time I use a Mason jar instead of a 'clear, empty bottle' from Russia.

After a poker game one night I came downstairs after everyone had left just to see if the Blessed Mother really glowed in the dark. She did and I was pleased.

When we moved to the farm I lost track of the Blessed Mother hanging ornament. I had graduated from St. Margaret and Father McCourt and was caught up in the eye-opening life of public school with lots more classmates, no school sisters of Notre Dame and no more cigar boxes full of money for the First National Bank up town.

They must have found another Presbyterian in the school to take care of those chores. My brother, Brian, six years younger than me went to St. Margaret as well. Maybe the job went to him. Poker games were many and often at the farm, and Dad's winnings seemed to increase when we no longer had the glow in the dark, Blessed Virgin Mary holy water font next to the front door. Nothing sacrilegious, and even though Dad was the one who agreed to adorn our Presbyterian home with the holy water font, I think he felt better when the odds were a bit more even.

======== 30 ========

Encounter With An Eastern Gray Treefrog

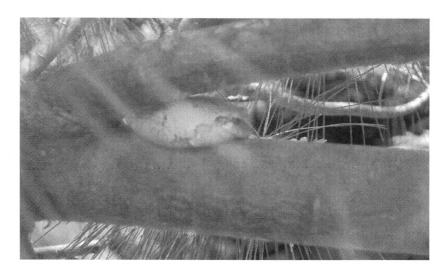

S ometimes the things we seek the longest and hardest forever elude us...only to pop up unexpectedly as if they were late for a date with our destiny. Well, you can quote me on that one because as in the case of the nesting Pileated's a couple years ago, less than twenty yards from my lane, another creature that I'd never heard of has suddenly appeared in the backyard, next to the fire pit.

Sitting with pals the other night a 'musical trill, a resonating flutelike trill, similar to the call of a red-bellied woodpecker,' boomed from a white pine bough above us. At first I thought it was Ken or Donna Scotten making a joke on me, but it turns out they were aware and somewhat befuddled by the sound too.

STH

Couldn't see anything but zeroed in on where the sound came from and sure enough, another call, shorter but just as loud. This time I stood on the bench and was able to see a tree frog gently folded into a bough.

Amazing colors blending in with the bark, the tree frog measured little less than 2 inches and remained motionless as I moved closer. A little white spot, just below the eye was the only thing I noticed to take with me to the Peterson Guide to Reptiles and Amphibians.

This morning he or she was still perched in approximately the same spot on the limb, with the light spot really evident below the eye. Some color shift is noticeable on the back and for the life of me, it's hard not to pick it up and examine the markings more closely, but something tells me 'no...don't touch the tree frog'...just leave it alone, savor the visit as long as it stays and be done with wanting to interfere, to be 'selfish' and put it in a terrarium or some other vessel of exhibit.

STH

In a way what I'm doing seems selfish, because I'd like to show the little gray tree frog to others. The other night Wolf Wallis came by, he's the guy who edits my copy for the *Delta Star* by the way...well I wanted him to see the little gray tree frog and we went outside, just after a light and well needed rain...but, no sign of the frog. With flashlight in hand I scoured the limb from tip to trunk...no sign. As we hopped down from the bench I couldn't resist playing a trick and as Wolf stood there I shined the flashlight on the ground and said, "Oh my God, you've stepped on the gray tree frog!"

He jumped back, befuddled and clearly shaken that he might have squashed this delicate creature...that's when I picked up a small piece of mulch and said, here's what's left of the little fella. He still thought it was a flattened gray tree frog...then realized it was a joke, on him...but still the thought occurred to me the frog will one day leave, just as he arrived. Yet, for that night, my frog friend was just being nocturnal and moving about in the dark. Sure enough, the next day, he was back in his familiar spot.

In the meantime, more visitors will see the 'gray' and perhaps enjoy the treat of seeing something of this 'earth' that they have never, ever seen before. That's the wonder of it all for me...to see something never seen before...in a natural setting, not on some two-minute TV spotlight or a rented DVD.

Spotting this small tree frog has once again humbled me in the pantheon of nature...how something so

delicate and mysterious shares space with the likes of me...how it sits so patiently, perhaps wondering what all the fuss is about.

Down in the marsh the spring peepers serenade each evening, but try to spot just one of them...as you get within a few feet they become silent and invisible...ah, the wonder of it all...

Doncha just wish some of these politicians were the same...rattling their spew, then when you get within a few feet of them, they disappear and become silent... makes you wanna get up close for a real good look.

========= 30 =========

All photos by Todd Holden.

Painted Turtles Emerging

E ach spring I look for painted turtles in the pond down in the marsh, alongside the floodplain that borders the headwaters of Bynum Run and Wysong Branch. Long before the lily pads erupt the stillness at dusk on the pond water reveals little, save a few gnats dive bombing the surface without destinations...or so it seems.

Recently Dee Dee Barnhill called to alert me of a great blue heron, injured along the banks of Bynum. Her son, Justin, was down by the stream and we noticed the bird wandering into the thicket downstream towards the beaver lodge. My thoughts were to leave the bird alone. So many times, well intended folk will try to 'save' an injured bird, only to cause more injury to the creature who is in 'fight or flight' mode to begin with.

Injured, the bird knows only to flee whatever is coming towards it...they are surviving in the world of Mother Earth...and that leaves little room for human intervention. For me it's tough to have to relate this to a young person, concerned with nature and it's goings on. But the truth is to ignore a 'gut feeling' for the sake of rescuing an animal that is hurt because 'it's the thing to do'...is wrong and unfaithful to the inner spirit of understanding our environment and the creatures that inhabit it.

Explaining to Justin, as I have to my own children, that to attempt a 'rescue' would only add injury in all likelihood...best thing is to let the heron alone, and if it's meant to heal it will get up on a limb to live or die. To take it to a vet is senseless in my mind, a shot of adrenalin or wrapping the bird sometimes will help, but usually the bird dies. They are so fragile with hollow bones, allowing flight and reduced weight, when they break there is little to be done. After all, when in danger a bird can fly away...the down side of that escape benefit is they are less durable.

As Justin left, understanding and accepting the situation, the old picnic table beckoned me to sit a spell and watch the water of the pond for a sign of a painted turtle. Sure enough, after sitting till my butt got numb a little snout appeared in the stillness, this lone face in the water assured me there was a turtle there, albeit just one...but greed is not welcome in the world of Walden and the experiment that continues here...one of 'live and let live'...unless they threaten my 'living.'

Never encountered a turtle I didn't like, 'cepting maybe a snapper or two who sometimes are just plain mean spirited. Wilson Ford told me once their only enemy on this earth is man...and they are unchanged in armor and appearance for eons. No sign of snappers... yet. So, satiated with the sighting of the emerging and diving painted, the trek back up the hill to the house was thoughtful and calming.

STH

Next morning I checked the shoreline of the pond with binoculars and noticed what looked like a dried out, dead shell of a turtle on the bank. A shimmery painted, neck fully extended was alongside, motionless. A good sign, now there are two painted's.

Bringing out the spotting scope I began searching the entire pond bank, and a third, fourth and fifth painted are observed along the banks...all shimmery from leaving the waters, save the one, motionless, dry, dull shell that I had seen before. This is all good, right before my eyes, painted turtles are emerging left and right.

Along the pond farther to the west, three more, much larger turtles are climbing up the bank, investigating, cautiously, slowly, with head sparkling like a waxed Chevy. Still the dull, dry, motionless turtle kept my scope coming back to it. Now there are nine painted turtles, where there were only two when this visit began an hour ago.

The larger shiny painted turtle is still alongside the dry, dull one, but alas, it appears now that the dry, dull shell had backed into the bank, because a head slowly is appearing on the downhill side, towards the water. Very slowly the entire head emerges and it dawns on me, maybe it's a female and she's laying eggs in the bank, and she's been at it quite a while, maybe since dawn and it's now ten o'clock.

Clearing the pond of spatterdock in the spring at Rustica.
Photo by Sam Holden.

Can it get much better than this? Rushing in to
scribble my observations, and back out again with the
scope, the dry, dull turtle is now at the water's edge,
motionless, as the sun bakes the bank...and all living
things thereon. Nearby, this visit reveals the great blue
heron, standing still on the far embankment. Surviving
for yet another day without the help of me or Justin.
Seems things are alright.

Whether the painted turtle was laying or not doesn't
really matter. She has moved...she's not dead...just dry,
dull and full of life. And the wheel in the sky keeps on
rolling.

========= 30 =========

Funny How Things Work Out

I drink way too much coffee...it's not a good thing after a triple bypass...we all know that. So I kind of shelved the Braun coffee maker on the kitchen counter, and opted to just get a 16 ouncer at WaWa every now and then, when I went by, or went to gas up the SUV. Seemed like a plan.

Well, it's funny how things work out sometimes for the good, real good. A few months ago I was asked by a pal to deliver the eulogy for his departed mom. It was tough. Eulogies are hard to do when you do 'em right and if you know the departed there's just a little more pressure to deliver the right words. For the family and friends in attendance, it's a little easier than sitting in a service listening to someone who didn't know the departed rattle on aimlessly about the merits of whomever the deceased is.

The eulogy was appreciated by the family and the next thing I knew there was a Tassimo coffee brewer on my steps. I'd never heard of Tassimo, and someone told me it was the ultimate coffee, tea, espresso and hot bev maker. Just one cup if you want, no brewing a big batch and drinking too much of it, or tossing it out.

Then I found out what the thing cost, and wanted to return it to my pal...way too much 'appreciation' for the eulogy I thought. The family would have no part of it, they wanted it that way. So I kept it. Wasn't quite sure

how to even operate the contraption, but I welcomed it
into my home...just like the stepladder I keep handy and
other replicas of a good life.

Well the next thing is getting my new pup, Dude,
from Daniel Lapp, up Fawn way. Now the pup is a
month here and he's learning fast...has sharp teeth...an
inquisitive mind and unbounded energy...after all, it's a
Jack. We're down to two 'late night pees' and for a while
four times a night left little sleep for me. Always hard
getting used to something new, but Dude has certainly
made himself part of the family and the heart is a big
place.

Frisco and Dude have gotten along well, and
everyone's activity around Rustica has increased. Things
are moving along. But as with little children, L'il Dude
gets up early, like 6 or a little after...and that means we
all get up, for the trip outside...about the time a good
cup of Jo would be great.

So I play with a few buttons and figure out the
Tassimo and try it...and man, it brews just one cup,
in less than 3 minutes...fresh and tasty Kona. As it is,
it's the coolest gift I've been given in a long, long time.
Technology can be a good thing and in this case, the
wonders of invention have brought a mem'ry of the good
old days back to life.

As we parade through the kitchen, all that's required is popping a fresh 'coffee pack' in the machine, turning it on, and heading outside. The brewed cup aroma fills the air and my senses...like a Colorado morning.

So, with the addition of a puppy and new sleeping habits for me, comes a wide awake feature in the kitchen to only add to the joy of getting up hours before I used to, and sipping coffee whilst I play with the pup. Good things happen...you just gotta be there.

========= 30 =========

My Pipes Are Froze...Can I Spend The Night?

That was the question...seemed real enough for me, and we've all gone through the frozen pipes, leaking water heater, busted radiator scenario...so I thought I'd use that request to conduct an experiment. After all, it was a way to break the monotony of a bleak, near zero degree day.

L'il Dude got me up at 7, which is fine with me... sure beats 4 am or 5...so I pull on sweats, cap, jacket, gloves, the whole schemer, and out we go...on a trek up around the tractor shed and back to the house...during which time he usually takes care of all his morning constitutionals...I say usually...but the cold weather has definitely affected his concentration out of doors lately.

Today things went like clockwork. Both Dude and Frisco took care of all manner of business and we headed briskly back to the house and warmth. Hearty or frail, it takes a while to thaw out the bones from this cold and that's when I thought of the frozen pipes. So while feeding the dogs I decided to have a little fun and called my daughter Mina...remember, it's 7:30 am.

"Mina, just had a couple pipes break, froze up, and it's gonna take a couple days to get things repaired...you mind if I come down and spend a couple nights at your place?"

Pause...then, "Really?"...umm...not real enthused, but also not bad, all things considered...I tell her 'no' I'm just kidding, just wanted to see what kind of response I got...we laughed...and she's off the hook.

Next it was Ron and Shirley Hooper, up on Quaker Church Turnpike...same intro, same appeal for a place to stay for a few days. Before I could finish, Shirley said firmly and flatly, "NO!" Okay, no doubt about that reply...then I told her I was kidding and she said, "Whatever you do, don't tell Ronnie." I won't...but maybe he'll read it in the paper.

Next call, to pal Billy Marshall, in Churchville... reply, swift and the best so far..."Not a problem."...and Billy knows I travel with two dogs...so he was on the money with his hospitality offer...of course, he has two dogs also.

Then it was my editor's turn, Pat Wallis, in Bel Air... his wife, Laurie answered the phone, it's now 8 am... temperature is up to 17 degrees and it's windy.

I ask the loaded question. Laurie's reply..."Sure, are you sure you want to come up here?" "Sure," I said. She then retorted by saying..."Emily (her eldest daughter) wouldn't mind sleeping on the floor, after all she's got the biggest room." Touché Laurie...a great sense of humor and kindness all rolled into one.

This is getting to be fun, revealing and highly informative.

Next it was locksmith Keith's turn...his wife Janet answers..."I guess so," she says. "Have you talked to Keith and asked him?" Very nice, and very much a happily married couple's way of lending a hand. Turns out, Janet's auntie Barb had a friend whose pipes were frozen the night before, so she figured 'why not?'.

Long and the short of it, it was a good way to catch a friend, or daughter, off guard with a hypothetical question, which involved sharing their space and time... and that's a big order these days...everyone has their own room, own TV, own computer, own cell phone... on and on...not like the days of this writer, when my brother and I shared a room early on...and we also shared a phone when we were young men about town. Kinda built character to get by on less.

We are spoiled by our comforts and space...and I love both...but when someone calls with a question that might lead to 'adjustments'...we all get a little tense...

Fact is, my pipes are okay...life is good and the weather is cold, hard and mean...it's winter...so it's an 'adjustment'...not like me moving in for a night or two... but an adjustment of mind over matter...and getting on with it.

========= 30 =========

Leave The Pods To Dry...And Then Shake 'Em

S ome people have all the luck, like cleomes
growing out of their mulch pile...a beautiful
self thriving flowering annual. They self seed, and
jump everywhere...just need a little bit of sun...and so
beautiful.

I had never heard of them before Donna Scotten
gave me some plants earlier this year...and now they
are thriving all around the house. Donna also gave me
Japanese iris, that are purple and smaller flowers...very
old plant. When they spread in the flower beds, the
blanket of color is fantastic. And some pink and purple
columbines...they too seed themselves and spread.

Also day lilies, the orange beauties that we see along
the side of the country roads, especially near streams
and bridges. Now they are just green for the rest of
the summer...Donna has promised me some 'perennial
begonias'...they come back every year, thicker than
ever...just need a little sun, but they also do well in
semi-shade...flowering pink

Over the years thanks to friends like Donna, Jim
Shackelford and Wilson Ford, I have been kindly given
some unusual and beautiful flowers, plants and shrubs.

STH

The pond is half covered with pink and white lily pads offering a Monet look as the sun sets. They were given to me by tropical fish farmer, Jim Shackelford when I built the house in 1984. From only a dozen or so lilies to over 100 today. They offer bass and bluegill a place to cover young fry and painted turtles as well.

Wilson Ford started me out with autumn and Russian olive shrubs...a colorful and sweet smelling plant that produces red berries for the wintering birdlife each year. From a couple bare-root shoots that Wilson insisted I plant, there are five huge olives situated around the house, and mockingbirds have staked them out each fall in a territorial maneuver guaranteeing their winter food sources.

Wilson also taught me to take scissors and a brown paper bag to clip seed pods of black eyed Susan's and glorioso daisies in the fall, and store them in the brown bag till spring, then spread the seeds for abundant flowering plants. At the studio I had in Bel Air, one entire side of the building was wall to wall with black-eyed Susan's...a weed couldn't grow in the thicket of Maryland's state flower.

It seems the best way to plant flowers these days, for me at least, is to plant flowers that propagate themselves each year...that way it's just a matter of keeping the weeds under control and letting nature take Her course.

Remember the Walden Experiment here at Rustica... mentioned years ago, as a plan of action for allowing nature to 'just be.' Today there are chipmunks and cottontail rabbits and new born black rat snakes. A good sign for sure.

Although snapping turtles are not my favorite reptiles, there was a six pounder in the stream the other day and I just let him be. If he'd have been in the pond where the painted turtles are, I'd have shot him. In the stream there was a chance to just observe for 40 minutes or so. With the huge, powerful, elongated head guiding the snapper along the rocks and scattering aquatic fry the words of Wilson come to mind..."on this earth, the snapper has but one enemy...man!" These prehistoric looking reptiles are indeed a formidable sight in a stream and afford no chance for wading and playing near them. They are aggressive and short tempered and I keep my distance.

The hummingbird moths are here too, resembling the ruby-throated hummingbird. They are interesting 'look alikes' that enjoy the flower beds at dusk.

Peaceful and with a little break in the sweltering heat of this summer, a low humidity day offers a clothesline full of sheets, pillow cases and towels.

Life is Good...the weather surely plays a role in it for me.

========= 30 =========

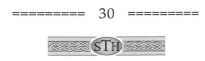

Why I Can't Watch One Of The Best Films Ever...

With one of the best opening scenes of any musical, a soundtrack that's impossible to forget, and a smashing 30-year-old Rita Moreno... Jerome Robbins and Robert Wise's 1961 transportation of Shakespeare's Romeo and Juliet's Capulet's and Montague's into rival gangs on the streets of New York remains one of the most visually dynamic and hotly colored musicals of all time.

It was the summer of '63 and the Capulet's and Montague's were alive and in love close to home. I fell in love with a lovely lady, dressed in red at a party hosted by a mutual friend. She didn't know me, or I her...we didn't dance, we didn't flirt...truth be told, it was love at first sight and that's no overstatement or cliché. It's the truth...we passed in the night, and went our separate ways...but for this guy, it meant calling every single Newman in the phone book the next day... all I had was her name.

Lots of hang ups, slam downs, interested parties... and then, finally, the Capulet family matriarch, Beatrice answered the phone when I rang up...I asked, 'is Ann there?'...and I heard magic, in her voice, "Ann, someone is calling for you."

A throaty response on the line..."Hello...this is Ann... who is this?"

STH

It's the Montague, name of Todd Holden... "I'm the guy from the party."

We dated and it was okay at first...as far as the parents were concerned...yes, those Capulet's and Montague's were powerful forces for these two falling in love. The magic of it all was in the innocence and comfort of falling in love regardless of religion. It didn't matter to us, but it sure did to the heads of the respective households.

Along comes West Side Story, a film we both heavily related to...we saw it over and over in the theatres at home and at the University of Maryland, College Park. We eloped and brought the dizziness of the film to live in our hearts. We beat the odds in this Judeo-Christian love match.

The university chapel tried to discourage our marriage. We couldn't go home because we knew what the answer would be. So we eloped in a simple living room at a Methodist minister's home in Upper Marlboro, Maryland. Ann's maid of honor was her boss from the Chesapeake and Potomac Telephone Company on New York Avenue in Washington, D.C. Her old boyfriend stood in as my best man and the ceremony was performed...albeit interrupted by an errant house cat wandering through the living room in the middle of the service.

STH

We both were scared to death as the few Polaroid's indicated. Me in an ill-fitting green khaki suit and Ann in her best dress. We lived out West Side Story, only with a happier ending than in the film. Happier then than I'd ever imagined. Being in love was so easy...for both of us.

We were alone in the world, without a lot of friends, and no relatives, except my brother, who I had told in secrecy the week before. The wedding date was decided by the college registration schedule, and the day before I signed on for my senior classes, we did what love dictated us to do.

Worries and problems were all gone, no one knew at home, and when we visited our parents we hid our bonds by matching signature rings hand-crafted by a jeweler in Baltimore.

The love story that is West Side Story is powerful stuff for this idle heart. I can't watch the film any more without crying...the tears well up sooner and sooner as the music and aerial view of New York City comes to the senses. It's just a movie, sure...but the meaning to two kids in love was such a fantastic parallel. We could live the 'movie'...we were Romeo and Juliet...and only we knew it...and it was all that mattered.

What was once love lives on in my heart. Maybe the reason it hurts to watch West Side Story is it is frozen in time, encapsulated forever in imagery that is sublime...a love that was sublime is more powerful because we lived it, we lived the dream of beating the odds.

========= 30 =========

Stone Walls Last With Care

Good Fences Make Good Neighbors
– Robert Frost

Most any drive or even better a walk along county roads will bring you to a direct link with the past that isn't found in tour guides or maps... the magnificent stone walls that farmers created hundreds of years ago and today some are still standing, and well kept.

Good neighbors indeed. A structured stone wall with mortar fronts the Dublin Methodist Church in Dublin, Maryland.
All photos by Todd Holden.

Back roads offer much to the leisurely traveler and Sunday afternoons are sure made for that. Away from the house on a clear day you can venture along some roads that verify county lore by names like Mahan Road, Carsins Run Road, Carr's Mill Road and Whitaker Mill

Road.   These roads are often named after millers who plied their trade as a 'go-between' among farmers when agriculture was king in Harford County.

Near the mills were fields rich with wheat, barley, clover and sorghum and when the fields were cut and baled or bagged the same wagons used to haul the grain to the mills were used again on the bare land to haul stones and rocks that would ruin cutting equipment.

It seemed each year, as the snow thawed, there was a new 'crop' of stone for the land owners to pick and haul away, usually to a ravine or ditch. They stopped erosion along stream banks and hillsides. It was land recycling at its finest, albeit hard work and time consuming.

While not a farming stone wall, this wonderful mixture of Peach Bottom slate steps and sidewalk with stone wall serves a purpose. This was found along Atom Road in Delta, Pennsylvania.

STH

Craig's Corner Road field stone wall with cap work. A classic refined county stone wall, keeping cattle in.

Rocks and large stones are fascinating in their own right. Sometimes covered with lichens, moss and various vines, they are survivors of the past. This must have been in the minds of those hardy souls who decided to make fences or walls along the dirt roadways so many years ago.

Thus began a tradition among some landowners that stands to this day, with the help of folks who are the current landowners. Sturdy, weathered and meticulously crafted, the stone bears witness to the weather and travel over many decades. Weathered stone speaks volumes, just as tombstones or survey stones throughout the land. Landmarks and places of interest are in abundance and are always worth exploring, but there is something very real about the layers and rows of stone placed by hand.

STH

Ronnie Knight's father instilled in him a love of the stone walls that line the west side of Carsin's Run Road, just north of Route 22, in Carsin's Run. When asked why he continues to repair and replace the stone that once fenced cattle he notes, "To keep it the way it was."

When purchased in 1941 there were 98 acres to farm, and tend to, and the stones were there then and continue to be a source of pride today to Ronnie and his wife, Jan.

"It's always on his 'honey-do' list," Jan notes, while Ronnie is busy fixing a broken drive belt on their lawn mower. "There are stone fences all over the farm and we try to keep all of them up, with the help of our son-in-law, Jeff."

"Vines and honeysuckle and saplings are tough on the placements and each year we have to cut them back or the root systems would just push the wall of stone over into the road," adds Ronnie. "Cars are often victims of the stone and vice versa."

"But it's the root systems of trees, weeds and vines that do the real damage, and if left unattended the walls would fall prey to environmental evolution," he added.

Where huge locust and persimmon trees have invaded, the stones are replaced appropriately and the beauty continues. To the Knight family the stone foundations of barns and fences surrounding them recall the pride and skill of those who settled here as farmers.

If you've traveled to Scotland and Ireland and seen the vast expanses of land lined with stone fences that determined land ownership as well as kept cattle, it makes sense that the many ancestors who came to this country and migrated from the south to Harford County would carry those agricultural traditions with them.

It was a true labor of love to build these edifices of a life with the land, every day, and every year. For decades, small families lived and cared for the land that offered so much in the way of survival and peace of mind.

As you drive along the back roads and take for granted a massive wall of stone, the weathered, smooth dark brown and black rocks may go unnoticed. It's when you take a minute to 'smell the roses' you also get a look at a page from the past that's still here.

A 'still young' stone wall along Southern Drive in Leeswood, Bel Air, Maryland.

STH

Along Carr's Mill Road, where the pavement was elevated years ago to keep cars from sliding into the stone fencing, the stones are in disarray in many places. Due to trees growing out and automobile collisions the remnants are in jeopardy. When roads are widened the walls are gone forever.

And so too is part of the pristine past we will miss forever…stone, rock, work and love made these monuments possible, and without caretakers like the Knights and many others, they will be lost along with much of the innocence of our land.

========= 30 =========

Times have changed since even 2004, when this story was first written. As happens with the ravages of time, Ronnie Knight's stone wall along Carsin's Run Road is now grown over with the vines, honeysuckle and saplings that he meticulously kept at bay. Precious memories, how they linger…thanks Ronnie.

A collection of stones picked from the field at Rustica Preserve.

STH

Appalachian Ballet

F ar away and over the hills where the sun goes down and the sound of a fiddle creeps in there's a place where bluegrass music reigns and the high tone harmonies beckon those coming down the country road. Pretty soon, the folks gather and the sounds of old time goodness and laughter fill the air as the players begin... and as they pick and sing others join in the dance...a dance I call the Appalachian Ballet.

Years and years ago a lady name of Hazel Ellis told me she clogged with a bunch of 'gooders' and how much fun they had. They were the Silver Eagle Cloggers and dance they did, here and there and all around. When the musicians took a break to get in on a 'fifty/fifty' was the only time there was no dancing on the hard concrete floor.

"Somewhere between your heart and mine, there's a window I can't see through."...goes the lyric and in the singer's face there's a window of history. It's a history of real life unfolding as it did hundreds of years ago as folks immigrated from Scotland, Ireland, England and Wales to the Carolinas and the Appalachian country. Then north to the green, less hilly fields of Harford County....the music came with them and to this day it's as real as it gets.

This dance, this gathering is a world unto itself, without fanfare, shunning publicity, seeking the sheer joy of making music and sharing a tradition steeped in heritage...worlds apart from the 'political correctness' of today's spirit of living.

The folks here are sitting, talking with one another, or getting up to move around a little...some slower than others. There are men with stiff, hunched backs who've worked the fields in their younger days when it was a 'seven day a week' job, from sunup to sundown. Back then, they were called tenant farmers and share croppers and if you don't know those terms you can look 'em up or better yet, go hang out at the feed store, welding shop or old hardware stores and see what you can pick up.

'Course the Royal Farm store sees the members of Appalachian Ballet too, from time to time. The men and women at these informal, clandestine gatherings struggle to walk and can't wait to dance. Fingers snapping and slapping inside and outside of loose legs the man in the plaid shirt keeps time with his body and the sounds he makes with it. A lady in a walker moves whatever she can to the tune being played.

Not every day do you see an 81-year-old man tear into a Snicker's bar, living wild and going for a sugar jolt, enabling him to get back to dancing and keeping up with his partner. Dark blue jeans and cowboy boots, blend into a fashion show with Nike and New Balance sneakers..."faded love...head over heels in love with you..." the music goes on and on.

"I Just Crossed the River Jordan" is especially powerful to me as it's played by a seven piece band... a blend of banjo, mandolin, guitar, fiddle, upright bass... no drums, just strings.

Looking around I see bandaged knees, a few folks are popping Advils and Aleves and it's true that some just come to sit and listen to the evening. They're eating hot dogs and sipping Coke or bottled water and are happy to see this 'live show' of talented folk who are tossing caution to the winds that blow outside across the fields. The movers and shakers aren't on any roll except the rhythm of the evening, but they'll dance a whole set before they take a break. Some of the sitters and lookers sometimes get carried away and get up to join the steady regulars for a dance or two...still the dance keeps on.

Old Flames Can't Hold A Candle To You

There is no alcohol, no riff-raff, no profanity, and strict adherence to the 'house rules'...no punks, no junk, no bad behavior, just folks acting like they've got good sense...like we were told to do when we were kids. The age difference is the only difference watching guys shyly go over to girls asking them to dance...the same as they did when they were teens, they still act the same and shyness becomes them in the innocence of social relief with the muse of fiddle and feet.

Some of the bands that play on stage are newtimers, anxious to share and a little nervous. Some of the bands have names while some are just makeshift combos, happy to oblige with another song. The only time there's a break in the dance is when an old-time gospel number is played and feet are still as respect is shown. Then, the banjo rolls and the guitar strums in a fast beat heightened by the fiddler's reel. The dance continues.

As the night rolls on, we see the shift from "Long Black Veil" to "Sittin' On Top of The World"…and the folks sing along in the audience as some get up to leave…an evening's escape from a life of living. It's not a late night crowd; it's a working class gathering of good hearted souls who share a love of their roots. Men are kind to each other and the women are treated with respect. Strangers smile as they pass and perhaps one last exchange of greeting before they move along. This impromptu choreography speaks volumes and the movement is real. They didn't learn the dancing at Arthur Murray and you won't be seeing any of them on American Idol…it's a different time, a different world… it's a secret, and it's the Appalachian Ballet. You can get there if you follow that sound coming across the hills and into your heart.

========= 30 =========

Cars and Innocence Lost

An enjoyable e-mail exchange with a buddy started out with a simple reminiscence of old vintage cars, like this 1957 Chevrolet Bel Air convertible, but turned philosophical when we thought of the sheer fun of driving back in the 50s...when cars were designed for comfort and design and owning one of these beauties was a way of life. Cars were pleasing to the eye in a different way than they are today.

Sure cars today are safer, but that doesn't mean they are as much fun to drive as they were back then...if that isn't true, then why do all the parades and conventions have 'classic cars' on display, being driven and appreciated?

Sam Spicer, a good pal and connoisseur of fine cars, has a 2002 Camaro and it's a classic, both on and off the track.

STH

Couple of months ago he told me to drive it and I was scared at first, then figured, 'heck, I've not been behind the wheel of a true muscle car' in a long, long time, so go for it.

I wound it out on a straight stretch of road and it was magnificent. The smell of the engine churning out awesome horsepower and thrust for just a few minutes was enough to satiate me for months to come.

Some comments on this special car by its owner Samuel Morgan Spicer, of downtown Hickory and Ady Road:

"It's not one of a kind by any means but probably a step above the average. It is a 2002 Camaro (the 35th and last year they were built, uses F body platform) with the factory SS performance package, a retuned version of Corvette's aluminum 5.7-liter V8 engine with forced air induction which pushes the power curve to 325 hp at 5200 rpm, with torque skewed as high as 350 lb-ft at 4000 rpm. The SS performance package also adds the forced air induction hood, unique spoiler, high-performance ride and handling package, 17" wheels, bigger brakes, low restriction dual outlet exhausts and Goodyear F1 tires. Transmission is the GM Hydra-matic 4L60E four-speed automatic. My car is probably in the 350 HP range because of the following options:

- High-flow air-box lid
- Cold-air induction package
- High-flow K&N air filter
- F-body smooth bellows
- Modular Loud Mouth exhaust system with tips

"These are part of what GM called the SLP package (Street Legal Performance). I changed the rear end ratio to 3:70 gears, also added a Granatelli MAF (Mass Air Flow Sensor) and I run consistently in the mid twelve second range at the drags, best is 12.46. Haven't been inside the engine as yet.

"For listening enjoyment a Monsoon stereo premium sound kit with in-dash CD player and as an option a 12-disc remote CD changer, AC blows cold air and I can drive it to the grocery store. Of course, living in the little paradise of Hickory I can now walk to the grocery store since a Redner's just opened up close by."

A force to be reckoned with. Samuel Morgan Spicer's prized 2002 Camaro. Photo by Todd Holden.

Okay, you may be wondering what all the magic in Sam's Camaro is about and it's simple really, he enjoys the entire product. Not only is the Camaro fast and beautiful, it's a reminder of a time when innocence was abundant in America.

America was addicted to something better than dope back then, we were addicted to grace, beauty, speed and sheer art...these cars were like seeing an original Van Gogh at the Philadelphia Museum of Art when the collection was on loan a few years ago.

More important, these cars speak volumes on where America was then...we were without the technology of today, the speed of information of today, the stress and pressure of today...but we were a lot happier and gentler and kinder back then. Sure, we worked on the engines in the evenings and Saturdays and then drove these well-kept machines so we could be seen, so we could compare 'notes' with our other car-buffs, and maybe to impress the girls. Still, the whole lifestyle was innocent, pure American living, where time mattered less than the road to get there...and we could get there fast.

========= 30 =========

Del Haven Cottages And Hotel

E arly ads for this landmark at the north edge of Bel Air at the intersection of Moore's Mill Road and Hickory Avenue were short and to the point...

"Strictly AAA ....Modern.....Phones....Delicious Food
Breakfast...Lunch...Dinner...Sandwiches
Open Year Round   23 Miles North Of Baltimore
U.S. Route 1   Bel Air, Maryland"

———————————————————————

"DEL HAVEN HOTEL AND COTTAGES - AAA
23 Miles North of Baltimore, Md.
Bel Air on U.S. Route 1, Md.
Modern Steam Heated Rooms, Private Bath, Garages
Large Dining Room, Excellent Home Cooked Foods,
Deluxe Furnished Cottages, Steam Heated
Beauty Rest Mattresses, Running Water, Community Kitchen,
Private Swimming Pool, Free to Guests - Showers
Gas Supplies, Handy to Churches and Amusements
F.M. Irwin, Prop."

As a kid, having just moved to a dairy farm outside town and on one of the many dirt roads in Harford County...I would ride my bike some two miles to have a Coke and pack of crackers at the counter in Del Haven.

The waitress back then in 1953 was a dark haired beauty name of June Martin...and her beau, Mack Jones, would usually be sitting at the end of the counter sipping coffee. To this 13 year old kid they were the perfect couple.

After the Coke I would ride my bike around the hotel, past the little cabins and over near the swimming pool, before heading home to the farm.

My dad told me stories of dances on the roof top of Del Haven, with musicians serenading couples dancing under the moonlight. Some times folks would dance until the sun came up...then go downstairs for breakfast. Today, you'd be hard put to find a place as glamorous as the Del Haven Hotel and Cottages.

From an airplane it resembled a Christmas train layout, with little stone walls, paths and bridges over a stream and plenty of benches for folks to sit and take in the country air.

Maryanna Skowronski, the current director of the Historical Society of Harford County, lives a little south of where Del Haven was.

She writes, "When the Wilsons owned the store, my sister, brother and I used to collect soda bottles from around town and construction sites and we would haul them down to the store to return them for refunds. It was a great place to buy Popsicles. We used to explore Bynum Run, next to the store. This was back in the day when parents could let their kids wander that far from home and not worry about them!"

None of these memories and reproductions of old post cards of Del Haven would have dug their way into my mind had it not been for George Donhouser, owner of Del Haven Service Center. In the past I have done photography for George and he asked me if ever there was a chance to locate some pictures of what once graced the corner directly across from where his service center now stands.

As the quest for photographs and images continued it made sense to me to learn as much from those who had direct dealings with the original Del Haven as possible.

An article in the *Aegis* newspaper, dated March 31, 1966, stated, "One of the oldest businesses in the county, Del Haven was built in 1923 by Felix Mack Irwin. In 1944, Mr. Irwin's brother, Eldon E. Irwin, who was the owner at the time of the Del Haven Hotel in College Park, Maryland, purchased the Bel Air version and managed it until 1952.

"The second story ceiling, over the dining room, boasts 20-inch steel I-beams, with 8 plies of wood on top of that. This was done so dances could be held on the roof of the second story during spring and summer months."

"The swimming pool coordinated well with the relaxing atmosphere of the quaint cabins and gravel pathways linking the entire complex together. There was a scale model of the hotel on the grounds and at one time a mischievous monkey lived in the little hotel, near the pool."

One such person who figured prominently in the history of Del Haven was Felix M. Irwin, and his grandson F.M. Irwin, III, who currently resides in the former Irwin home, about a mile north of Bel Air. With the help of the Irwin's and another lady, Mrs. Clara Wilson, the piecing together of the story of Del Haven began to take shape.

Ironically it was Clara's dad, William Martin Roberts, who, while living in the mountains of Ashe County, North Carolina, was approached by none other than Felix M. Irwin, who was touting Harford County 'up north in Maryland' as the place to go with your family and settle and do good." Little did Clara realize that one day she and her husband, John W. Wilson, would give up their farm and purchase Del Haven.

Mr. Roberts listened carefully to Felix and pulled up stakes in 1927 and moved the family to Harford County where they purchased an 89-acre farm on Route 543, Ady Road, a few miles north of Emory Church and south of Pylesville. Clara met her future husband while in the seventh grade at Highland School. She later attended University of Maryland School of Nursing, graduating in 1943. She and John were married shortly after. A few years later, they bought the family 'home place' on Ady Road and with 2,200 chickens started selling eggs and taking care of her dad. Meanwhile John, a natural-born mechanic, was working as a test-pilot and flight engineer for Glen L. Martin Company in Middle River.

A close brush with death on a test flight in 1949 left John and Clara with thoughts of starting their own business in Harford County. So it was again that Felix M. Irwin came into play when the Wilson's agreed to purchase the already established Del Haven in 1952.

"Eggs were selling for $1 a dozen, and I loved the home place...I wasn't that pleased when John suggested we sell my beloved home place and buy Del Haven. He was very convincing...every day by 5 o'clock in the afternoon, all 12 rooms were rented, and most of the seventeen cottages were occupied," Clara pointed out.

"Del Haven was also one of the major 'stopping off' points for travelers between New York and Florida. It was really a bustling business for both of us sitting on a little over 2 acres...there were fifteen employees, including three cooks, a handy-man, gardeners, five waitresses, and three maids for the cottages. A lot to take care of," she added.

"I had one rule for the place," Clara points out, "No shenanigans, no gambling." Harford County at that time was a 'dry county' meaning no liquor sales at commercial establishments. No drinks with meals, or if you wanted that you went to the Kingsville Inn, over the county line.

Clara and John's big Del Haven venture was rolling in high-gear for about three years, open all the time, every day...by dinner time the place was usually filled up...the "No Vacancy" sign lit.

Then the Delaware Memorial Bridge opened, and traffic north and southbound could make travel faster... and some of the hotels, like Del Haven slacked off in terms of volume. "The patrons thinned out after the bridge opened. Some nights only five rooms were rented...we had to buckle down and cater more to the local people," she says with a sigh.

Clara continued..."We had to let help go...I never dreamed I'd be waiting on the tables. One night a girl I went to nursing school with came in with her husband. Here I was, with an R.N. degree, and here she was with her 'doctor' husband. So, I said, "It's o.k., we own the place...and that seemed to make things better," she adds.

STH

Ultimately we had to close the kitchen, and just kept the lunch room open. John made a trip to Elkhart, Indiana, where mobile homes were being made, and drove back with one, set it up on the property and started selling them...at one time there were ten mobile homes for sale, brand new, and ready to go," Mrs. Wilson recalls.

Del Haven went from an enchanted oasis and prosperous hotel and cottages, to a grocery store, gas station, mobile home sales and then, a used car lot. Around this time John started mapping out plans to demolish the buildings and build a shopping plaza. He and his sons, John Jr., then 20, and Steven, 19, took a 1957 Ford front-end loader and a chain-saw and began dismantling the main structure in the Spring of 1966 and the end of Del Haven as many townspeople and travelers knew it, came to pass.

"We took it down bit by bit. It took about a month, and we were allowed by the county to burn the wooden parts of the building, far away from the highway. No one got hurt either," remarked John, Jr. from his home in Florida.

Dale Neeper, of Bel Air remembers..."As a small child, my recollections of Del Haven are rather skewed compared to people who are older. However, I do remember going to Del Haven to get ice cream. Their chocolate nut sundaes were the best. We also would buy 'hand packed' ice cream to take home. I remember my oldest brother playing the pinball machine while eating the ice cream that he would buy on a regular basis.

"We knew everyone who worked there and the folks at Del Haven knew just about everyone who came in to the store. My Dad would stop on Sunday afternoons to buy an El Producto cigar to smoke as we took our family Sunday ride. Del Haven was our 'go-to place' when we ran out of something like bread or milk.

"My brother Roy mentioned the pool. That is where he was on the day WWII ended in the European Theater (VE Day). I remember Roy being sent to Del Haven to pick up bread, ice cream and, sometimes, beer. The ride down Moores Mill Road in those days was very exciting. He loved to drive my Dad's car to Del Haven sometimes squealing wheels and 'hot rodding.' More often than not, he would also run into some of his friends who were also at Del Haven picking up needed items."

Today, as you look across Hickory Avenue where it turns into Conowingo Road, you see Del Plaza Shopping Center...anchored by the 7-11 Store and eateries, a tailor and dry cleaning shop, a fitness center, florist and hair salon. At the time of the razing of the original buildings, Mr. Wilson had said, "I anticipate a drug store, laundromat, barber shop, beauty shoppe and a food market." Giving way to the future, the Del Plaza property was sold by the Wilsons in February 2002. John, Sr. passed away March 31, 2008.

One of the first stores to open was a 7-11 market and a two-bay service station. Different proprietors and establishments followed. One of the original cabins is still standing today, across Conowingo Road from the original location. At one time it served as a home for Coy Greek Irwin, a brother of the founding Irwin's. He was a barber and cut hair there.

I had heard that 'Greek' owned a Stradivarius violin and he often could be heard playing it on the little porch of the cabin. Family members know of him 'playing the fiddle often but think the Stradivarius story is mythical.' Greek was sometimes tormented by the kids who came to Reuben's, a drive in restaurant adjacent to Del Haven. He was known at times to fire a shot from his .22 over the heads of hecklers hanging out at Reuben's and to shoot out floodlights on the parking lot at the popular drive-in.

Today, a little bit of the story survives in that little white frame cabin. Some of the cottages were of brick construction, others were wood frame.

Felix M. Irwin, Jr., known as "Buddy Irwin" passed away in 2002, and his son is the current resident with his family north of Bel Air on the original home-place of the grandfather Felix Mack Irwin, who died in 1969. His body and some of his family are entombed in a large white marble crypt in Mount Zion cemetery near Fountain Green.

The last remaining cottage at Del Haven. Photo by Todd Holden.

For those who recall the 'good old days'...what
was once a landmark is gone and like so many
other landmarks the Del Haven Hotel and Cottages
disappeared as the times, economy and demands
changed. Its day is gone...but not forgotten. And thanks
to George Donhouser the name Del Haven carries on in
the name of his service station on Conowingo Road.

Life is all too fleeting, and as you walk and breathe in
your own particular time the present is what's real and
your surroundings are what are vivid. A quick call to the
take out shop, an even quicker stop at the 7-Eleven to
pick up that something you have to have and time sure
does move fast. These recollections may help slow the
pace a bit and the snapshot of a simpler time...certainly
not easier, just less baggage...may offer a glimpse into a
time and place almost forgotten, but not just yet.

========= 30 =========

Good Brothers Are Hard
To Come By

My brother, Brian Holden, after winning first place for the Best
Street Custom Rod, Washington, D.C., Car Show, 1966. The car is a
1933 Chevy 5-window coupe with original all-steel body.
Photo by Todd Holden.

Sometimes, an 'only child' has a tough row to hoe...
seems those with brothers and sisters talk about
fighting with their siblings, and there are often bouts of
envy and estrangement, then in the final tally, they are
still 'family' and most times 'close knit.'

Brother is a term of endearment as well as a
biological reality. "Brother, can you spare a dime?"
reflects the use of 'brother' as an intro from a pan-
handler on the street who is looking for a handout.

STH

"Oh Brother, Where Art Thou?" was a great film, dealing with the the travails of three pals, unrelated, but totally brothers in the keenest sense of the word.

I had a brother, John Brian, for 20 years. He left this world in his twentieth year and I had a brother no more. Friends who were close became my 'brothers' and many are still close to this day...some have fallen out with me and left my friendship, but they are still brothers in a 'family tie' way.

Good buddies are 'brothers'...we do all the things real brothers do...there is no 'obligatory connection' where we have to be pals, or share Thanksgiving dinner with... the neat thing about 'pals who are considered brothers' is that there are no ties that bind, nothing but the sheer friendship and wanting to share it with each other.

Men who have served our country in the armed services consider friends made among the ranks, brothers in arms. Banded together in a common good, a cause. From basic training to wherever they are called upon for service, these boys to men learn to trust their brothers with their life. That's about the most dedicated form of brotherhood anyone could sign up for.

Blood brothers are few and far between. Jimmy Rinehart and Tommy Broumel and I all became blood brothers during a ritual of a boys club we formed long ago. The ceremonial initiation involved cutting or using a straight pin to bring blood, and then mixing it with

The Boys Club on the occasion of Jimmy Rinehart's 7th birthday.
Top row left to right, Joannie Childs; Betty Coale; John Wilson, Jr.;
Unknown (possibly Sarah Coale). Front row left to right, Brian;
Jimmy Rinehart with brother Gary on lap; charlie Broumel.
Photo by Mrs. Alma Rinehart.

that 'brother,' thus sanctifying the union of pals through
thick and thin.

Some consider the guys on their bowling team
'brothers' and the list goes on. Point is, brothers don't
come and go...they last, stick like glue. When a 'brother'
has trouble or runs into some bad luck, brothers are
alerted and word gets out. Family brothers or Pal
brothers, they step up and come to the aid of the hurting
brother. No words need to be spoken, no paybacks are
necessary. Just the reassurance that a brother has your
back helps to weather some dark storms.

STH

Of course, brothers can cause some mischief and at any turn there may be some shenanigan pulled just to bring some excitement to the situation. Pranks and hi-jinks played on an unsuspecting brother are actually part of a time-honored tradition...sort of a ritual hazing into the rite of brotherhood. Still, true brothers won't let the prank go too far. Being a good sport is part of the initiation too.

Having brothers and being a brother is something I know of. I'm quite proud to have had a family brother, though I miss him strongly every day. Yet, I'm also proud to have a strong posse of brothers who have had my back as I've had theirs. The feeling of love and concern for our brothers depends on the depth of the weakest link...surprisingly the bonds of brothers who are just friends and acquaintances is far stronger than most folks realize...about the strongest glue I know.

========= 30 =========

Part Of The Family Here At Rustica

"If a tree falls in the forest, does anybody hear?"

Rustica Home after 23 inches of snow fell in the winter of 1994.
Photo by Todd Holden.

So it was the other night, the winds clocked on my Weather Channel monitor at 60 mph as cold and warm fronts collided and Mother Nature wielded her force. With a powerful gust, the landscape was altered and a special Colorado blue spruce went down beside the house here at Rustica.

Sometimes trees are as much of a home as the people, pets and furnishings inside. This was a special tree since it was our first Christmas tree when we built this 'passive-solar-envelope' home in 1984. We moved in, my family and pets, in October of that year.

Our first Christmas was special in this new home made of pine siding and lots of glass. The man who helped me with digging the foundation, grading the lane and surrounding soil was Frank Grafton and he happened to have a tree farm near Hickory.

When time came to pick a tree Frank volunteered one of his larger blue spruces. My son Sam and I went up to get it in our pick-up truck. We had shovels and burlap to wrap the 'ball' in...or so we thought.

We picked out a nice 8 footer and next thing I knew Frank was cranking up his backhoe and winching the base of the spruce. I knew for sure this would ruin the tree, but held my tongue since it was a gift.

As soon as we got the nearly bare-rooted spruce home we all pitched in filling a wading pool with soil to cover the roots and give the large tree some support. My daughter Mina carefully tied clothesline to the top and lashed the tree to the upper deck over the sunspace.

We straightened the tree up just fine and decorated it with all the trimmings. Christmas in our new home became just a bit more special and Blue Spruce added to our happiness. Some more soil was added as the watering settled more around the roots. Still, I thought it would not make it, not the way it was taken from the earth it was growing in.

All through the holidays that first Christmas the smell of fresh spruce permeated the sunspace and inside

the living quarters. It was a fine way to start our life here, with such a mature evergreen. There were always 'live' balled in burlap Christmas trees when we lived in Leeswood and it would be the same here at Rustica.

Sam would dig the holes for each year's evergreen in late fall when the weather was warmer and then cover the hole till after the holidays. There are fir and spruce from every year surrounding the house.

Darn if the Colorado didn't make it through the season, and when Sam and I planted it outside the den window beside the parking area it made it through the first summer. And so it made it through twenty-four years until last night when high winds took it down, snapping it off at the roots and laying it over like some large green ship.

Sadly, I looked it over tonight, at dusk, and it was like losing a big part of my home. Laying there, looking it over, not a trace of bagworm or any disease...this was one healthy blue spruce. As I gazed at it lying prone on the earth, I pictured it still upright and majestic. She was an old friend to the landscape of Rustica and part of the family that has grown up here.

It will lay there till the ground dries out enough to either drag it down to the woods margin or be cut into sections to move. Either way, I don't want to mess with it now, just doesn't seem right, and since it didn't tear anything up when it toppled I'll spend a little more time saying goodbye.

It's got the best aroma, getting into the boughs the traces of old mourning-dove nests and robin nests are evident. This old babe made it when no one gave it much of a chance. And when big winds hit Rustica on Father's Day 1994 we lost a couple of flowering crab trees and one Quanzin cherry tree. Blew one of them about 40 feet across the lawn...those winds came from the north. The big winds last night were all from the southeast and they also took down a big tulip poplar tree along the lane. It, too, was snapped off right at the ground and shattered like a toothpick. That tree will have to be cut up and used for firewood by friends.

Me...I'll knock off some of the soil around the spruce roots in a few days, and little by little come to grips with the fact that it has to be removed and make way for something else, maybe.

Every time I mowed the grass here I had to shy away from the low boughs of the big spruce or suffer the scrapes and abrasions on my arms, back and legs, as I tried to get as close as I could trimming around the base.

That seems small change now that the big, significant evergreen is gone. Not as bad as losing a pet, but much the same in losing something that has made it this long, here, as part of the family. The view out the den window, watching the sunset won't be the same that's for sure.

========= 30 =========

Another Link With...
The Good Old Days

So many of the touchstones from days gone by are 'gone by'...for good, and that's not so good. As a kid growing up between Delta and Bel Air and farms in between there were certain things that impressed me a lot. The Pylesville 'creamery' was one, and the Delta slaughter house was another. Don't know what the fascination with these two places was, both being along the Ma and Pa railroad line, but whenever I was nearby, there was an attraction to go and see what was going on.

When old men gathered at a hardware store, like Sidwell's in Delta or McComas Brothers in Bel Air, a kid just had to hang around and absorb whatever was being said. Places where youngsters like me could just be on the fringes of what the 'big boys' were saying was a thrill and highly educational. It was also a ritual of acceptance and another passageway to growing up.

Feed mills were also places of great learning from men of the land who worked with tractors, cows, hayfields and silos. That's what turned me on. When I was seven, I learned to drive a Farmal Super C tractor, pulling a hay wagon that we loaded with rocks picked from a freshly baled hayfield.

Another special place for me was the post office. Going there with parents and grandparents was a special treat. Everyone knew everybody and you'd stop to gab

with a familiar face on the latest happenings. The mail brought news from faraway relatives and then there were the magazines...colorful stories fresh from the 'outside world', sometimes the only source other than the radio when something happened. There were photographs in the magazines and that brought even more excitement to a kid's eyes.

The post office could also be like a courtroom or a police station...there was an element of high drama in these government buildings. Not everyone had a sense of humor in any of these places. The ones who did enjoy a laugh were special people to kids like me. Of course, the post office had 'America's Most Wanted' posters... mug shots in black and white on hard white paper, these were big time criminals. I never saw anyone I knew of. Always wanted to swipe one of the wanted posters, but never did.

All the post offices along the Maryland and Pennsylvania railroad were similar in their smells, of oiled floors and musty brooms, and cats, God almighty, so many cats in every one of them...cats were a calming effect I reckon, and for sure they kept the mice in check. There was always a saucer of milk at the rail station in Bel Air. Cats also were targets for pranks, just to watch them take off in fear when someone lit a firecracker or tossed a soda on one. I must admit I took part in a prank or two, just for the learning experience mind you.

STH

Post offices were usually situated alongside or near the rail station, or in the case of Pylesville, a grocery store near the rail head. That all changed when transportation modes changed. Today there are big, fancy post offices. They moved the old post office in Bel Air right out of the heart of town and built a huge, almost heartless building mingled in with the big mall and shopping district. No more walking to the post office for those who live in town.

The Forest Hill post office operates out of a renovated store that once was Klein's Department store. The smallish post offices are a lot more friendly and folksy than the big town ones. Just a touch of the old days... and yes, I still have a P.O. box there. Now that I'm retired, part of my daily routine in making my rounds is to swing by the old post office and see what's up.

A trip to the Street post office recently brought back memories of old time local places where news and events were talked about and shared. Unlike the big post offices around the area Street offered up a bulletin board chock full of local news.

This is a classic link with the ways things used to be done, and still are done today, with all due respect.

'Lost—Jack Russell'...when I inquired, the postal lady said, "Oh, I have to take that one down, the little fella was hit by a car."

'Illusionary Magic of Rick'...some enterprising talent looking for work.

'Yamahas...50 and 125 cc'...but remember, you have to have a place to run them!!!

'Cleaning Services'...a whole lot of folks are getting into the housecleaning business...a definite sign of the times.

'Limo Services'...'Marine Contact...for local Marines wanting to get together'...'Cactus Willie's'...'Horse Boarding'...'Pampered Chef'...'Colorectal Cancer Screenings'...'Unfinished Picture Frame Moldings'... 'Woodstoves'...'Hired Hand Landscaping'...

All kinds of offers of work, products, notices of the missing, lost and found...all there on the wall in the hallway of the Street Post Office...just think, there's rarely a long line, the folks behind the counter are friendly and efficient, and if there is a bit of a wait, you can read the bulletin board and learn a little about the place you live. If you're lucky, you might run into someone you know.

========= 30 =========

Don't Ask Questions, Just Enjoy

Without a doubt, there is a blessing of birds here at Rustica. For some reason, and it's beyond me, there are more birds, doing more things, than I can ever recall. There are lean years, when many of us don't see a lot of hummingbirds or there aren't as many robins, but the variety and volume of these winged creatures are a beautiful scenario to behold.

This year started out with the arrival of red-breasted nuthatches, more than ever before...and they stuck around, no doubt enjoying the beef-kidney suet I placed to entice them. Smaller and similar to the white-breasted nuthatches, they made a colorful addition to the birdlife gathering daily at the black-oil sunflower feeder. There is only one feeder, and its placement is strategic to ensure a good look from the den window.

The hummingbird feeder went up early in the spring...the first diners were downy woodpeckers, darting between the nectar water and the suet feeder as they prepared to nest and raise families. Next was a male ruby-throated hummingbird, arriving in late April, and thankfully the feeder was primed and ready.

Before I saw a female ruby-throat there were American goldfinches. Never noticed them before on a hummingbird feeder, but it was interesting to see the variety of birds enjoying that one little plastic feeder full of sugar water.

Outside the den window are rhododendrons and azaleas and a giant weeping Norway spruce. In the rhod a pair of robins started building a nest with much of the grass clippings from the first mowing in the yard. Nest construction was underway, and I had a ring-side seat to see the way it was built. Mud, clippings, long stringy weeds with both male and female hard at work. The layering of grasses was meticulous and planned out over the course of a week...then the mating flights began.

The robin's nest is less than six feet from the humming bird feeder and a little farther from the Droll Yankee feeder. On rainy days the nest is actually solidified, binding the mud and grasses into an adobe.

Out on the deck are the ceramic bird boxes that Karen McKenzie made for me years ago. They are decorative and creative and never had anything inside them except twigs from wrens to keep other birds out. Each year I clean out the twigs a couple times and just enjoy them. This year a Carolina chickadee took one over and lo and behold a mossy nest appeared with eggs inside. The second ceramic house is now being occupied as well. There is one on each end of the sixty foot deck...and the constant chattering blends in well with the wind chimes at special times when a stretch and nap are in order by me and the dogs.

The pileated woodpeckers are less noisy this year, but are nesting down along the wood margin between the house and the pond. They have not been back, as close, on the lane as they were three years ago, when we

all watched as the three young fledged. That old tulip poplar was dead long ago from a lightning hit when they bored out their nest. This past fall it blew down in a windstorm.

They really must know what they're doing.

New roofing was installed on all of the bluebird boxes and the battle to keep the wrens out, continues, but that's old news and never ends.

There seem to be an abundance of cardinals this year, so many males flitting about, darting in and out of the Russian olive and hemlock. Truly the female cardinal is one of the most gorgeous birds in flight.

Every now and then I rake away all the sunflower hulls from under the feeder and scatter them across the driveway allowing other birds to gouge out little insects that are attracted. Sort of recycling the seeds from start to finish, and usually it's the finches and chipping sparrows that dance around scaring up something to eat.

Every single day the vultures appear, making lazy circles in the sky and then heading into the marsh and over to the next open field at The Vineyard farm, north of me. Sometimes the turkey and black vultures settle down, and land in the field to pick apart something. What it is I do not know. Only when a white-tail deer is injured by a car, and limps onto my place and dies is there a feeding frenzy with the crows and vultures.

That's fine with me because once you've had L'il Dude and Frisco tear into a rotting carcass and then come bounding in the house reeking of foul stench can you appreciate the work of Mother Nature's undertakers. It's amazing the work they do, efficiently and completely, providing they are left alone to do it.

Today the early morning songs fill the air around the house. A happy and peaceful lyric of many birds. There are no more Manx cats roaming about, just the two pups and they are 'user friendly' for birdlife...well, almost. When Frisco sees a hawk gliding overhead she barks and chases after the soaring bird. It's a throwback to when we raised peafowl and banties and sometimes a Cooper's or Sharp-Shinned hawk would swoop down and pluck one of the peeps from its mother and carry it away for dinner.

That didn't sit well with Frisco, and to this day, even though there are no more peafowl or banties to dine on, she does her best to discourage 'fly overs' by hawks and vultures.

All in all it's a fine environment for birdlife and most wildlife in general...it's the old Walden Experiment continuing...just getting along and living in harmony with nature. Not always easy, and one day when I'm gone the tranquility of Rustica may be no more...but that's a ways away and doesn't interfere with the beauty of what is here today.

========= 30 =========

Reflections On Turning 70

Turning 70 is a state of mind as the author reflects.

J uly 4, 1939, my Mom and Dad were bouncing me around as they drove through Washington, D.C.... Dad later said he had hoped I'd be born on the Fourth of July...a little firecracker...the first born...well, the road wasn't rough enough and I held out till the next day... born in Sibley Hospital in our nation's capital.

Now, 70 years later and I'm still bouncing around, usually from funeral homes where my pals have been laid out and doctor's offices where my pals are trying to cure what ails them. Viewings at Harkins' and McComas' are just about the closest thing to informal class reunions as I can get...if they just served some appetizers and wine it would be a little nicer. A few more of the old friends would turn out and we'd have more stories to tell...maybe the 'where are they now' list would be shorter, even if it turned out to be on the other side of dirt.

Things have a way of slipping up on us as we get along with age...we mellow out a bit...some more than others...others not as much as they could. We don't complain, because we never liked being around whiners as we were growing up. We try not to do the things we avoided when we were half this age.

Someone once said, "If I'd a knowed I was gonna live this long, I'd a taken better care of myself." Really? Would we? Nah, don't think so. When you really look yourself in the eye, in the morning gazing into the mirror...would you really change much about the way you've lived your life? Maybe some things, but not all things...we are what we are...and the good that men do is oft' interred with their bones.

It's the little things that change for us...not because of us...sort of an involuntary change, here and there...some little changes that maybe we don't even realize, but our friends do...and maybe they don't mention it.

For example...when I was working, every day was a fresh shirt, pants and socks...retired...well, I take off my shirt and pants when I get home from errands... and if they are clean, I hang them up and wear them the next day...I do my own laundry, don't mind that, but it seems a waste of energy and water and detergent to do lots of cloths that don't really need it...socks? I gave up wearing them when I retired...can't stand socks...in the winter I have to wear the 'supphose' kind with my Redwings...otherwise, no socks...less laundry...and a feeling of freedom.

Whenever I would go into someone's home, I always removed my shoes...a tradition my mom started when I was little...'take your shoes off, and don't track mud across the kitchen floor!' she would admonish. Seemed like a good idea, because the half 'tar heel' in me feels better walking around bare-footed.

Okay, so the little things that indicated I'm getting older...like getting out of bed in the morning...first off, I sleep a little later...usually till about 7 before I get up and at 'em...letting the pups out, watering the red maple beside the deck and putting on the coffee. I ache a little more in the knees especially and so far not the neck, back or arms. For that I'm forever grateful.

When I watch a good film, a classic like "Out Of Africa" or "One Flew Over the Cuckoo's Nest" ...near the end of the movie my nose starts stinging and sometimes I cry...don't know why, I just do...the sadness hurts more now than it did 25 or 30 years ago when I first saw those films.

When I see a deer or dog along the road, dead from being hit by a car, I want to turn around and get the carcass away from being run over and pulverized. I've stopped on Route 40 to drag a beaver off the road and heft it over the embankment into the swamp near Edgewood. Such a majestic creature, dead because a trail it was used to taking is now blocked by 'Jersey Walls'...and I wonder, why can't the road builders leave little gaps in those concrete barriers to allow wildlife to pass through in treks they've made over the years?

Can't fix that, but it hurts me to see death like that... and again, my nose stings with the preamble to a tear.

Little kids crying, not whining, makes me wonder what I can do...makes me think of raising my own kids and what I used to do...and what I do now with grand-kids...maybe even men have 'motherly instincts' when it comes to children...our own or those of others.

The computer age has been great for many of us older folks...it keeps us up to date and in touch with the world, our friends and our minds are kept sharper...more so than reading a book I think...I read the messages and news on the computer screen...and still read books...and write better because of both.

That's just my opinion of course...you might feel different...but at this age, I don't really care as much about what others think...because of where I'm coming from...not a place of competition or a mission to reach a goal...just getting along each day, doing what I think is best and keeping my head about me.

When I was younger, older folks to me were characterized as saying what they felt, telling the truth, no matter how much it may hurt, and being wiser in life's messages. This is true...mentors like Wilson Ford, Winfield Mitchell, Coolidge Spraker and Cleve Coldiron sometimes spoke harshly but always honestly... sometimes I didn't know how to take their criticisms but always got over it, in time, and then realized they were right...but they didn't pussyfoot around trying to sugar-coat things so the medicine would go down a little easier.

And that's where I am now...sometimes it doesn't pay to pussyfoot. Just say what's right and the things that are on your mind...you'll be better for it and whoever you're with will respect you more, later.

Of course there are my children...and their children... and it's different now because I'm no longer the dominant player...they are...and well they should be... but of course we, as the 'elders of the pack' still feel the need to be in 'the game'...and luckily for me, Mina and Sam keep me in the game, but use me 'sparingly'...it's a new game now...and like the Baltimore Colts, they were great, but are no more...and new players are in the line-up...and I like the 'new team'...I like being in the game, if only for a few plays...still in the game...

Is the reason we don't get what we ask for because we don't ask for the right reasons?

In many ways we are the same as we've been all along...watching birds, enjoying nature to the fullest... that's all the same and getting better each day...it's the other little things, like our health, our finances, our ability to go out and work, get paid...save up a little extra cash...they are the reminders that we are entering another phase of life...we still have so much in experiences...and so little time to share it.

========= 30 =========

These Rocks Are On Fire...

Swale and rocks by the end of the first day of 'picking.'
Photo by Sam Holden.

Whoever would have thought my son Sam would ask if we needed to pick rock from the soybean field? As the earth exhales its winter breath, these rocks push up from the ground while the field is clear and it's easy to find the bigguns that can wreak havoc on John Magness' aging International 1440 combine. Sam journeyed up from the city where he lives and works and was ready to lend a hand to an old tradition. When I was 12 or 13 one of the jobs on Southampton Farm was picking rocks from fresh baled hayfields.

So the same hayfield is today as it was in 1953... once a part of Southampton it is today the proud home of Rustica...my home and fields...with the Walden

Experiment and all manner of wildlife, flora and fauna...
and with the coming thaws each spring come the
eruptions of rocks along this ridge running west to east.

Each year, rocks of every size, shape and color spring
forth. When it came to fortifying the eastern swale of
the overflow from the pond, Sam thought the field stone
would make a lasting and attractive bulkhead. On his
free days, we have gathered stones from the field while
we can see them and hauled them down to the swale. So
far it's grown in size to over twenty feet long and about
three feet high from the water's edge.

Across from the stones are two big logs that were
felled by the resident beaver colony, making a natural
sunny area for the painted turtles and an occasional
great blue heron. Zooming by at any moment are
the visiting pair of wood ducks, along with a pair of
mallards and a pair of Canada geese.

Spring is popping with procreation, seemingly more
so this year than in years prior. Beneath the deck are
families of rabbits...unseen, unheard, yet setting L'il
Dude and Frisco crazy as the scent of their traipses
beckon like Chanel #5 to a bachelor. In the midst of these
natural dramas are the field stone that have popped up
with each rain, making their presence known.

The stones come up each year, with the heaving and
belching of the fields after freezes and thaws. It's like
clockwork each spring, and as much a tradition as fact
of nature, we gather them, and more importantly, 'use

them' in walls around the driveway, free-standing stones of this place, for this place, just in a different 'place.' For these rocks and stones are like living and breathing artifacts of life on the land and, depending on their shape and bearing, demand to be displayed, much as an artist arranges the landscape he paints.

I can no longer lift the big ones, found in rare spots along the lane or exposing themselves along the ridge by the paulownias grove. Such aged, weathered stone, of no particular significance other than they have survived... weighing more than a hundred pounds and aching to be placed around my home...in various places of honor.

The smaller stones in the fields are just as important when it comes to fortifying the pond and sink-holes where the pond-diggers filled with earth, and now, after 25 years, rain and underground water from the marsh have eroded the earth and created sink holes big enough to break a leg or fall into.

With the tractor we fill the bucket-loader to the capacity that the front tires will withstand and dump them along the pond edge or into the sink holes. Recycling the stones from one life to another. And never in my wildest dreams did I ever think I'd hear Sammy offer to pick stone and help me haul it to the pond to reinforce the over-flow swale. Sam has been on the move in so many other ways and his world is filled with activities far removed from the simple chores carried on at Rustica. Yet, to hear him say, "Let's get some rocks," tells me he respects the traditions...he gets it.

He wasn't as ardent a fisherman as he has grown to be...years ago, with his pop-pop Newman he fished now and then. Then he discovered girls and that was it for the Zebco and night-crawlers. Then, about four or five years ago he re-discovered the pond and the big fish in it. When it filled in 1984, Wilson Ford and Winfield Mitchell passed largemouth and smallmouth bass and blue-gills along to me from Bush River.

Alive and well, they spawned and re-created until they pretty much made the little pond their home forever...the fish and lots of painted turtles, an occasional great blue heron, two families of wood ducks and the everlasting lodge of beaver, close by. Many times I've written columns on the old picnic table that Stan Watson made many years ago...it has lasted well, and for fishing, picnicking, or writing it's hard to beat.

So it came to pass that Sam has joined forces with me in preserving and maintaining the pond and marsh. This love of the land and respect for nature is not something that is taken lightly. The yearly exercise of gathering stones is more than a tradition, for the secrets of the rites of passage in honoring the land are shared between father and son. Gee, who ever would have 'thunk it'?

The more I see it the more I like it...not for what it is, but for what it meant to both of us creating it.

========= 30 =========

STH

A Fitting Farewell To A Great Pup

The preamble to the passing of Koda... my son's dog for the last 17 and half years came with preparation of the gravesite, on the north shore of our pond here at Rustica. As is sometimes the case, Sammy, my son, arrived without notice and went straight to work digging a grave for his pal.

Saying goodbye one last time.
Photo by Todd Holden.

Earlier in the week he had built a suitable casket for her...such was his love and deep felt pain of seeing her suffer in the past year...slowly going downhill physically, but still sound mentally. The last time I was with Koda Girl she struggled to get up to greet me, and sniff my pant legs for tell-tale traces of Frisco and L'il Dude.

As always she sniffed and wagged her tail...this time more feebly than ever before. She stood on shaky hind legs and then after proper greetings and petting her gently, she lay back down near Sam's desk at his studio.

As the week progressed, the coffin was completed and ready for what was coming. Sam's partner, Donna, and he prepared a last meal for Koda...white meat of chicken, from a rotisserie bird. The past week her vitals were slowly shutting down but she was able to eat a little of her favorite meal.

The morning after, Sam and Donna arranged for the vet to come by. With deliberate conviction, they set about with the grim proceedings carefully chosen for Koda's departure. The inevitable was upon them, yet they had prepared the best they could. Like many of you reading this, the rest is what happens when we have to put a dear member of the family to 'rest' when there is no hope of getting better. It was a soft Saturday weather wise, and I had gathered the tools to cover the grave and taken my pups to the pond to wait for the arrival.

We toasted the old girl, with Glenmorangie and Maker's Mark and laid her to rest. At one point L'il Dude put his paws on the side of the coffin and looked in at Koda...it was a moment I'll never forget.

We cried and shared a story or two about this wonderful pal of so many years. I learned that Koda's mom was an abused dog, tied in a back yard and neglected, later rescued by a social worker who was visiting the family on 'human matters.' Shortly after she was rescued the dog gave birth to eight puppies and adoption requests went out to all her friends, Sam among them.

Originally Sam wanted to give the pup to me, but at the time I was in no shape to take on that responsibility. Providence smiled and Sam kept her...she became Koda, K-Girl or just plain K. The wonderful journey of man and dog began and the two were inseparable. Just as Frisco and L'il Dude are so much a part of my life, so it was with Sam and Koda. At one point, when Sam had to travel with work, she was hostelled up here with me, then me and Frisco and of late, with L'il Due making it a foursome, three pups and one lug on two legs.

When we let our pals know of Sam's loss, it never occurred to me they would want to share their grief and obvious understanding of losing a pal. Some of the notes that came to Sam revealed the terrific love others have for creatures that solely depend on us, yet give us strength in understanding.

Holding court in humble fashion, Koda enjoys the sundown at the pond.
Photo by Sam Holden.

From John Adams, York, Pa..."Sam, sorry for your loss. Anyone who has ever had the pleasure and honor to be chosen as a sidekick to our wise and noble four legged sages can feel your loss. My advice, after the proper time of mourning, head straight for the SPCA, maybe you can be once again chosen..."

From Tina Hill, Delta... "My heart goes out to you and Sam. Our pets definitely are a part of our family."

From Holly Daiger, Bel Air. "We love them more, when they are gone, and you'll always have them in your heart. Remember the good times, and let them fill your heart with joy!"

From Bob Chance, Darlington, "No words needed... Give Sam a hug for me."

From Mac Lloyd, Churchville, "Lovely place of rest for an old and trusty friend...I appreciate your caring efforts even though I didn't get to know Koda. (But I do know you, so I'd expect no less.)"

From Sam Spicer, Hickory, Md. "Sorry Bud, Life sucks sometimes."

From Shela and Herb McComsey, Crawley, W. Va. "So sad when we have to bury our beloved pets. Amazing how those little critters

STH

grab ahold of our hearts and pump all that loving into them. Beautiful resting place."

From Wolf Wallis, Bel Air. "The friendship of a dog is a sacred trust. Those eyes...it is like they know more than they will tell and have somehow been here before. The love...it's completely and undeniably unconditional... that's why we give it back. Pals for life."

========= 30 =========

On a recent visit to Koda's grave, L'il Dude, Frisco, and me. Photo by Sam Holden.

100 Years Of Scouting

My Dad's Boy Scout Troop in Delta in 1927 was #326 and when my time came, I was 14 years old and my Scout Troop in Bel Air was #777. Scouting was a big part of our lives. I'm certainly proud of my achievements and thankful for the exposure and lessons that being a Boy Scout brings. Scouting recently celebrated 100 years of the 'adventure and continuing the journey' and the Boy Scout life is a journey worth celebrating.

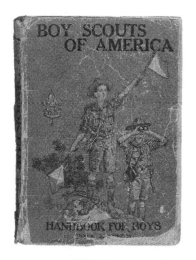

Lessons of life between the pages. My Dad's Boy Scouts of America Handbook For Boys.

In Dad's Boy Scouts of America 'Handbook for Boys,' the third page lists the following statistics... "Gwynne LeRoy Holden, of Delta, Pennsylvania, age 14, height 5 ft. 7 inches, weight 115 lbs., a member of the Flying Eagle Patrol of Troop No. 326."

His 'Scout Handbook' sold for 40 cents and was in its thirty-sixth printing...a run of 100,000 copies. At that point, 2,892,871 handbooks had been printed in the United States. The original handbook was published in 1910 and subsequently the editions and qualities were updated and continued. The original edition was a run of 68,900 copies and a second run of 4,500 copies had to be quickly printed to keep up with demand.

In the preface it states..."The Boy Scout Movement has become almost universal, and wherever organized its leaders are glad, as we are , to acknowledge the debt we all owe to Lieut.-Gen. Sir Robert S.S. Baden-Powell, who has done so much to make the movement of interest to boys of all nations."

The handbook is illustrated with drawings and lists camping, bugling, business, botany, bee keeping, blacksmithing, bird study, aviation, art, astronomy, athletics, architecture and agriculture among many other studies as ways of earning the merit badges. Wow...what a rich offering for the young scout preparing for life!

In my days of scouting I reached the rank of Second Class and was working on becoming a First Class Scout when my interests in the farm we were living on took precedence with both my time and desire to make rank.

I had made one requirement for First Class, that of earning and depositing at least two dollars in a public bank. Alas, it was trying to manage the General Service Code, also known as The Morse Code, handling at least sixteen letters per minute that was my undoing.

I had also completed the fourth requirement for First Class, making a round trip alone to a point at least seven miles away (fourteen miles in all), going on foot, or rowing a boat, and writing a satisfactory account of the trip and things observed.

Turns out much of my life is indebted to that requirement when it came to journaling and writing articles such as this column as well as my photo-journalist days from 1966 to 1972 when I served on the editorial staff at *The Aegis*. While these are achievements I can say were directly influenced by being a Scout, the moral and ethical lessons I learned as a young trooper are ingrained in the way I live my life. Bottom line, I'm a richer person because I was a Boy Scout.

I was lucky in the summers to camp at Broad Creek for two weeks at a time. I loved every minute of it and met some life-long pals there.

While Dad made First Class, the only one in our family today to reach the rank of Eagle Scout is my son-in-law, Todd Horn, who did his scouting near Mount Solon, Virginia.

The late Marshall Heaps would always let me know when one of his sons made Eagle, no small achievement in any person's book.

And so it is that 2010 is the 100th Anniversary of Scouting in America. Many of our friends and relatives have passed through the scouting program and have been chosen to receive the "Good Scout" award.

Many of our fellow scouts have earned 21 merit badges on their way toward the rank of Eagle Scout. Large goals are achieved through small steps, a lesson that has fortified many young men on their life journey.

The small troop I belonged to was sponsored by Saint Margaret Church in Bel Air, and our Scoutmaster was Hon. Harry St. A. O'Neill. We had just a few scouts in our troop but we camped on Camporees at Harford Glen and Broad Creek with the best of them. Harry's dad, Senator Howard S. O'Neill was the recipient of the Silver Beaver award in Scouting and was responsible for donating the outdoor chapel at Broad Creek scout camp.

So it was that the O'Neill family introduced a group of kids to scouting and the adventures that go with it.

For this I am grateful, because it dove-tailed with my life on Southampton Farm doing chores, romping along streams and forests and camping with my brother under the stars, and occasionally rain.

If you think about Scouting, take the time to lend a 'thank you' or support to the local troop in your area. You'll be doing the Boy Scouts a favor and yourself as well.

Keep in mind the motto of the Boy Scouts..."Be Prepared"...not a bad bit of advice for these times.

========= 30 =========

A Cold Night In March, 1970

Photo by Todd Holden.

Working as a photo-journalist during the turbulent 60s and 70s had its moments of terror and fear, as bombings and fires raged with anger of blacks and whites confronting each other. One such night of fear and anxiety came in Harford County as the H. Rap Brown trial was to open in a few days.

The trial never happened, in Bel Air...after a car with two black men inside exploded along Route 1 and Tollgate road, while the town was under 'lock down' because of threats the police received from supporters of Mr. Brown.

The story I wrote and the photographs taken were shared with Time-Life magazine in New York.

From Time magazine comes this account of what happened next:

"Two black militants were killed when their car was blasted to bits while they were riding on a highway south of Bel Air, Md. The dead were Ralph Featherstone, 30, and William ("Che") Payne, 26. Featherstone, a former speech therapist, was well known as a civil rights field organizer and, more recently, as manager of the Afro-American bookstore, the Drum & Spear, in Washington. Both were friends of H. Rap Brown, whose trial on charges of arson and incitement to riot was scheduled to begin last week in Bel Air. Reconstruction of the car's speedometer indicates it was traveling about 55 miles an hour when it blew up.

Police believed that Payne had been carrying a dynamite bomb on the floor between his legs and that it accidentally exploded. A preliminary FBI investigation supported that theory. Friends of the dead men contended that white extremists had either ambushed the pair or booby-trapped their car, perhaps trying to kill Brown. But police pointed out that Featherstone and Payne had driven in from Washington without notice, cruised around Bel Air briefly and seemed to be headed back. That assassins could plot and move so quickly defies belief.

Although Featherstone had not been known as an extremist, friends said that he had grown markedly more bitter in the past year. Police cited a crudely spelled typewritten statement found on his body: "To Amerika: I'm playing heads-up murder. When the deal goes down I'm gon be standing on your chest screaming like Tarzan. Dynamite is my response to your justice." Brown, meanwhile, was nowhere to be found."

For me that night will forever remind me of fear of the unknown. Like the fears we all share today, back in 1970, fears of racial unrest and upheaval were on everyone's minds. I had worked that night along the roads leading into Bel Air, the county seat...and had stopped by the Armory in town for a coffee with some troopers. Nothing was going on, the town was quiet, which was good, so I headed home.

As I drove my VW bug past Saint Margaret church I heard a blast that scared the life out of me and yet, I turned around in the roadway and followed my senses onto Bond street and southbound on Route 1. The smell of death was in the air as I came on the scene...body parts hanging in trees along the side of the road, fuel and car parts strewn along the highway...police and fire crews arriving one after the other.

Life as it was would never be the same in this sleepy little town...and racial outsiders, agitating even had the black population of Bel Air upset and afraid of what would happen next. Most of my friends in the black

community were confused by all the outsiders picketing and demanding the things many of the locals already had...jobs, respect and homes here in town.

It was a job of a life-time for me, fresh out of college with an English literature and history degree, and given the chance to write for the biggest newspaper in Harford County...beyond my wildest dreams. Plans were to teach in the county, and the pay for me would have been $5000 a year. The editor of *The Aegis* was John D. Worthington, III, a goodly man, a bit of a rounder, rough around the edges...so we got along fine.

The only thing he said to me when he hired me on was, "Write it the way you see it...just put down what you know as fact and we'll never have a problem." That was it...no sermon, no booklet on the 'whys and wherefores' of *The Aegis*...just get out on the scene, tell it like it is, and play it right down the middle.

There's more to the story, but recently seeing the photo of the 'Featherstone' car was enough to conjure up some memories of the long, strange trip to where things are today in my life.

And sometimes, when I come across some things from the past days, I feel they should be shared, to better understand one another...and myself.

========= 30 =========

Love Is No 'Annie Oakley'

Life is a circus and we are all under the big top. Some of us are performers while some of us are the roustabouts. Townspeople come to watch us perform, and the circus animals do our bidding. During the days of the Wild West Show, that most magnificent and American of circuses, Annie Oakley would shoot holes in playing cards that were tossed in the air. She was so accurate that her name became known as a free pass, to describe a complimentary ticket that had been punched so that it could not be resold. In the real world, there aren't any free passes.

The loves we've had and the loves we've lost...we're the lucky ones if we've loved and been loved in return. Unconditional love is a term that gets thrown around a lot these days, and it doesn't apply as easily as it is uttered. Yet, while I understand it now, when I was full into a love like that I'd never heard of the expression.

Seems words sometimes define themselves in our lives but not in our printed or spoken words. It's as though we are freely given to them. The love of pups has been written about here often and from the heart. The unconditional love that exists between my pups and me is an unwritten code of acceptance, of undeniable gratitude. Funny, when there is no other love in a life, we can find it in the most unexpected of places.

The love of children and grandchildren is a special love, a love of understanding and acceptance. We bridge generational gaps when the love of a child grows into the love of their 'new families' and their children, on and on. That's life under the big top.

Love is ever-changing and always a part of our lives, either as it flourishes or in its absence. Love is there as a black hole or it thrives as a field of sunflowers, radiant and enthralling. It is always in our hearts. Love is sometimes unrequited, sometimes spurned, or even unfulfilled, yet we seem to always yearn for it.

On a more local level, if we're lucky we 'love our jobs, our co-workers'…we 'love the Ravens'…we 'love a cold beer and crabs'…we 'love a good time'…we 'love life'…we 'love the smell of fresh mowed grass'…we 'love the scent of sheets' as they dry outside in the sun.

More prophetically, love is that whole life under the big top, perfectly described by the end song on a Beatles album…'And in the end, the love you take is equal to the love you make.' I firmly believe that, it's a mantra to my life.

We often are not loved in return, sometimes that's just the way it goes, but we still love on nonetheless. We learn not to waste love on things that are unworthy or selfish or mean spirited. Our love is meant to be shared, to be sent outward from where it resides in our hearts…

STH

and sometimes, that's hard to do. Still, we keep in mind..."If you want something you've never had, you've got to do something you've never done."

In the end, we're all in the big top. The calliope plays the song of love and we enjoy the moment. Love is always in the air, yet we still have to grab the ticket... and of course, we know that love is no Annie Oakley. We got a complimentary ticket into this place but, there's no 'free ride' when it comes to matters of the heart. We spread as much love as possible, get back what is given, and the rest just seems to happen.

========= 30 =========

Pain Of Irrelevance

We do the things we do because we have to...
or we want to...or maybe just because we are
able to. If we're lucky we do them well, and are duly
rewarded with a good life, a nice place to live...a good
family, good friends and friendly relatives. We embrace
life. When we get up each day the sun is shining even if
it's a cloudy day. We are not bothered by 'things to do
today'...we are anxious to let the dogs out, make the bed,
shower and hit the road...either to a job, or some task
that we have taken on because now in retirement, we
have the time to. It's just the way things work out.

When we are moving from childhood dreams and
schemes to the education of either college or the school
of 'hard knocks' we are busy making a life, a career, a
family, and nothing else really matters. We are driven in
those years after high school...right 'slam bang' through
middle age and on. If we're lucky and healthy and
fortunate enough and with some help along the way,
we make our way in this world. Along the way we also
just might make a couple of right decisions in who we
live with and how we live with them. In that regard, the
poets are right...it's the journey that becomes us.

It is a road we cannot easily look back on as we make
our way. The things we do are so 'of the moment' that
we can only look ahead. Yet as we age and mellow,
it is good to look back once in a while and that is
usually prompted by someone we knew along the way

mentioning things that we might have forgotten. The
sheer excitement of reminiscing is something those of
us up in years all cherish. Pleasant memories are good
to conjure up. Even some of the bad times that set us
back when they happened but eventually worked out are
now good stories...they are all there in that big memory
bank...waiting to erupt and shower us with nostalgia.

As we get on in life we have more time to reflect
and recall the good we've done, and try to leave the
mistakes behind. Our minds are a wonderful machine
when it comes to this...we tend to forget and forgive
the bad times, and savor the better images of love and
fun. Negative thoughts give way to peaceful reflection.
Thank God for that gift, and pity the souls who can't
invoke that good spell. There are always the terrible
memories like the death of a brother or loved one...surely
they are indelibly etched in our spirit and will never be
forgotten...and well that should be. Those memories are
different and demand special care...the sad experiences
help define our journey and lend gravity to the levity.

Amazing as it may seem, our friends are our memory
bank file and 'keepers of the flame' of all we've said
and done. Places we've been, events we've shared, an
adventure we went on and somehow the details have just
blurred with time...thoughts we just plain forgot about
for years. Then, on a chance meeting and conversation
with someone, a recollection comes up and it all comes
back and may even be embellished a bit.

At 70, it seems more often folks remember something I've done that to them was really interesting, funny, exciting, brilliant, dumb, riveting, uncanny...well you get the idea. I'll own up to what I remember, but I may not admit to everything...suppose it all adds up. For the most part, my life has been an open book...sharing your life makes it that way. As we grow longer in the tooth most of our life really is like a book of chapters that go on and on. Writing these chapters is why we are able to remember some of 'the better ones'...and diminish the lesser ones. We truly do have artistic license with our lives and our chapters should all be well written. The more creative we are the longer the shadow of our passing. The more riveting the event the stronger the recall...so it goes with all of us.

Then comes the time we 'retire' from the hustle and bustle of daily work and find a hobby or some other routine to occupy us. Then there are those who hang up the hammer and just wilt and die. Lots of folks I've known and greatly respected have retired and passed away in less than two years. Can't understand that one, just seems to be that way.

Others among us 'retire' from one job, only to take on new things and adventures, but it's never the same, because it was so easy to 'jump in' when we were younger and more able-bodied to work with a huge purpose. The drive to 'keep doing' comes from our learning how to embrace life when we were younger. My first jobs were when I was 8 or 9 and pulled weeds in Dale Coale's garden near my home. My reward was

vegetables Mr. Coale grew and my mom would help
me put them in neat rows in my Radio Flyer wagon so I
could pull it around the street and sell the vegetables to
neighbors who didn't have gardens.

That's just the way it was, and that drive stayed with
me most of my life. It's the way many of my generation
were raised. It wasn't a curse or punishment, it was
good, it taught a lot about how to get along in this
world. I don't regret a minute of it. I think folks like
Dale Coale and others gave me a chance to see 'self
worth' and satisfaction at an early age and it held me in
good stead all of my life.

We see these treasures manifest in our own children
and grand-children as we move along on our own paths.
As they learn to embrace life, perhaps sharing something
we've learned along the line will sustain the relevance a
bit longer. They are building their own memory banks
and writing their own chapters and from time to time we
can lend a hand with what goes in their book.

There is one little badgering problem though. As
we try to keep up in a downhill stroll physically we
mentally try to make up for it. We are aging in the body,
slowly, surely. We try to avoid the 'aging' mentally, and
fight to continue to be relevant. The mental will go too
and the book will be written, but as long as the journey
continues we must embrace life and do what we can.

STH

Irrelevancy is the enemy. No one among us wants it, so we keep up to date on what's going on around us. The problem is we cannot do the magical things we did as we matured...as we traveled the path from peddling vegetables in a red wagon, to working, raising a family and 'amounting to something'...along that thread we were hard to beat. We were 'winners' and we shared the loot along the way, we shared our lives with those we loved.

Friends pass away, it is the way it is, and we are a little lonelier for that. We make new friends, usually younger, so it's not quite the same, but it's good. We keep going, loving what we have, knowing we will lose another pal some time up the road and not worrying if it's us. Something tells us not to worry.

And while we live on, we are more aware every morning when the sun comes up that maybe we aren't as relevant as we once were. We want to be, but we are not...and we don't accept it fully, because in our own ways we are relevant. It's just we don't always feel that way and we have to work hard to keep that thought out of mind.

========= 30 =========

Appreciation
Farewell To An Old Friend

Steve Nelson, outside the Holly Hills Motel in Aberdeen, November, 2009. Photo by Todd Holden.

W e're never really ready for the news and then when it hits the shock just numbs us. Yesterday, I drove by my old office at *The Aegis* building on 10 Hays Street and turned onto Pennsylvania Avenue as I've done so very many times, looking to the right at

the back porch of the Risteau Building, to see if Steve (Nelson) was standing there waiting for the bus to take him and others back to Aberdeen.

So it was that at that very time, around 2 p.m. September 25, 2012, paramedics were responding to a call of 'an unattended death' on Law Street in Aberdeen. Steve had been out the previous night, came in about midnight and was not seen alive again.

His brother Stanley broke the news to me telling me the Aberdeen police said there was no sign of 'blunt force trauma' or 'foul play' tentatively setting the cause of death as a heart attack. The body was taken to the State Medical Examiner's office for an autopsy.

The end of the trail comes to a truly well-known, gifted, character of our county. In some ways Steve's passing, alone, in his own bed, maybe was the way it was meant to be. My son said when he learned of Steve's passing...'Well dad, this was a long time coming.' He was right. Steve Nelson was a man I was privileged to know, as I'm sure there are others who feel the same. And maybe even more who didn't like him. What he lacked in conformity he made up for in soul.

Always curious, I was intrigued by 'off center folks' of Bel Air. I would often see Steve hitch-hiking along Route 22 heading to the community college. No matter what the season there he'd be, 'thumbing' with his big wool coat, and long, tattered scarf, beard blowing in the breeze.

STH

Steve, at home on South Atwood Road, Bel Air, 1995.
Photo by Todd Holden.

He was harmless for sure...a loud mouth at times, belligerent at times, needing a bath lots of times, needy at times, broke most of the time...and always wanting a sip of scotch whiskey.

I took him food and loaned him money. And know what?...He would re-pay me most of the time. He would stake out the little studio I had at 30 East Pennsylvania Avenue early in the day. When I'd pull in there he'd be on the front steps. Or I'd slip into MaMa Nick's on Main street at the end of a darkroom day and there's Steve at the bar, sitting with horse trainers from Pons' farm.

Or Steve would 'just be' around town. There were many who came off as too good to speak to him, or acknowledge his presence...I can only ask them what's the harm in speaking to anyone, regardless of their station in life or manner in which they present themselves?

The story of Stephen Douglas Nelson, born December 7, 1950, is one of many complications, and ironically, if he'd ever been arrested and sent to jail, the home he lived in might still be in his family. There were detractors but, strange as it seems, police and locals alike were sympathetic to Steve and his beleaguered brother Stanley.

Steve's parents, Stanley and Ertie Walls Nelson, owned the home at 16 South Atwood Road. It was left to his brother, Stanley Nelson...so Steve would 'always have a home'...but Steve let some bad types stay in the

house. Neighbors complained, finally the Feds came in,
raided it, and took the house...Stanley was left without
his rightful inheritance...the United States Marshall
Service sold the property for $80,000 to a Bel Air
insurance agent on April 28, 2003. Stanley could never
afford to buy the house back in today's market, not that
he would if he could.

Steve's days as a controversial figure on South
Atwood had come to an end. He moved into the Holly
Hills Motel, in Aberdeen. During an interview with
him, we caught up with each other and of life in Bel Air
without Steve and Steve without Bel Air and his old
home.

From there he bounced from group home to group
home in Aberdeen, never to return to live in Bel Air,
his hometown. He was in failing health, suffering
with emphysema and poor nutrition. His smoking and
drinking didn't help either, but as many know, smoking
and drinking are the plague of the down and out
sometimes.

Bel Air's current chief of police is two years younger
than Steve, and grew up knowing of Steve very well.
"After his mother died, Steve became a total nuisance.
Between January 2000 and August 2001 there were 75
police responses to his house. Everything from dog
fighting, fun fire, disorderly persons, drug dealing,
medical assistance. I told Steve and Stanley this had to
stop; it was affecting the entire neighborhood. There
were many warnings, and finally, our department issued

a 'zero tolerance' policy,"
stated Chief Leo F.
Matrangola.

"Steve would let
anyone into his home, and
one of them was a police
informant, and when we
learned of drugs being
brought to the house,
Judge Angela Eaves
signed a search warrant
and we carried out a raid
which led to his arrest and
others. The house was
forfeited to the Federal
Government, and on June
5, 2002, the U.S. court

Steven Douglas Nelson.
Photo by Todd Holden.

noted the owner did not file a claim on the property, he
defaulted, so it went to auction," according to the chief.

Chief Matrangola, however, was sympathetic with
Steve's predicament. "Steve put people in fear, because
of his abnormal behavior, irrational personal behavior,
unsanitary conditions of the house, criminal elements
hanging out there constantly, just how much could the
neighborhood take, after all the warnings something
final had to be done. Steve never sold drugs, I know
this, and if he had and he had been sent to jail for it, the
house might still be in the Nelson family," according to
Matrangola. "It is unusual the way it turned out, but he
didn't help matters any."

STH

His older brother Stanley refers to him as 'Steven.' When Steve signed his name, it was all one word, 'Stephenelson.' There was also an older sister, Joyce.

"When he was 7 years old my parents gave him a ukulele for Christmas. He hit a couple bad notes, then took it outside where we were shoveling snow, and smashed it to bits," Stanley recalls.

In the tenth grade Steve was sent to the Maryland Training School for Boys because of truancy. While there he learned to box. He served his time and in 1970 his mom bought him a VW beetle. Soon after, he was involved in a serious accident, hitting a tree, totaling the VW and landing in the hospital in a coma for 22 days, according to Stanley.

"After the recovery from the wreck is when it all started, the paranoid-schizophrenia and poly-substance abuse. Steven was going to the college and had over 60 credits in sociology. Then Dad died in 1988, and Mom in 1991. Their will stated a 'life time living right for Steven to stay in our home until he died. It was my inheritance for taking care of him," Stanley remembers.

While there are many who would just as soon cross the street rather than meet eyes with Steve, there are also some folks who have a fond remembrance of Steve:

"I remember Steve. I used to talk to him when I was like 16-17...but it was hard, because I think so many people

my age back then used to torment him. Twenty years later, when I was coaching wrestling at BA, I used to invite him to matches, get him in free and hook him up with concession stand food."

Keith "Watty" Watson.

"Poor buggar."

Dave Hanson
Bel Air, Maryland

"I have many memories of Steve; we always considered each other friends. When my sons were small we would sometimes go to Fortunato's for pizza and we would often run into Steve there. He would sit with us and share our pizza. Our friend Joe has a line – 'ain't no guarantees' – so goes the life of Steve, we can only be grateful for our blessings and help others when we can. He who stands on tiptoes is not steady – laotze."

As ever, the most venerable,
John "Rooster" Adams,
York, Pennsylvania

Word of Steve's passing will travel through the
community and this article is but a fond farewell to a
friend. Many others have already contacted me to share
their thoughts about Steve and no doubt his legacy will
continue.

The infamous "Maggie Mae" connection must also
be told. Steve used to proclaim that he, "Bel Air's own
Steve Nelson" actually wrote the song for Rod Stewart.
The song is a huge piece of music and I guess Steve used
the line to wow the gals early on. "Steven actually dated
a girl by the name of Maggie Mae, and all the stuff in the
song was about the two of them," recalls Stanley. "At
the time Steve was playing bass in a rock band called
Blues British. He was playing with all older guys. They
played a lot in Baltimore, could have gone big time, but
it just fell by the wayside."

I tried to nail Steve down one day to confirm if it
was really true. He said he'd forgotten he'd written it.
Another mystery in the darkness that was Steven Nelson.
Far from being a shadow figure, Steve Nelson emitted a
genuine light of humanity that we all could learn from.
May his light shine on.

========= 30 =========

Rules For Clotheslines

A view of the oft used clothesline on the side yard at Rustica.
Photo by Todd Holden.

One of the joys of living where I do is having a clothesline to dry all laundry on. A day like today, sunny, little wind, is perfect for sheets, pillow cases, jeans, shirts, skivvies, and all manner of socks, handkerchiefs and even jackets and sweaters. Seems as though the elastic lasts much longer when garments are air dried.

The sunshine and breeze offer a scent that is unmistakable and hard to beat for the sheer smell of cleanliness. When the weather is foul, I will dry shirts, pants and skivvies inside on the large center beam of my home. Living alone affords the use of the beam for laundry, and just like the clothesline, the drying is fine, and just has to be taken in when company comes by, or in the case of outside, when the sun starts sinking in the west...a couple times I came home, forgot all about the clothesline and next morning had to re-arrange the clothes on the line to dry out again.

There are a few rules for the clothesline and you might have a few to add to the list...if you've ever seen an Amish home clothesline, you are seeing a true 'masterpiece of laundry drying'...long ropes, usually running from the home to the barn, on a couple of pulleys.

Basic Rules For Clotheslines
(If you don't know what clotheslines are, better skip this)

- Wash the clothesline before hanging any clothes - walk the entire length of each line with a damp cloth around the lines.

- Hang the clothes in a certain order, and always hang "whites" with "whites," and hang them first.

- You never hang a shirt by the shoulders - always by the tail! What would the neighbors think?

- Wash day on a Monday! Never hang clothes on the weekend, or Sunday, for Heaven's sake! I break this rule regularly, since a sunny day, after a week of rain, might afford the best weather conditions for clothesline drying. Hang clothes when the sun is shining, regardless of the day.

- Hang the sheets and towels on the outside lines so you could hide your "unmentionables" in the middle (perverts & busybodies, y'know!). On the other hand, I hang my skivvies and towels first, near the north end of the clothesline, the larger stuff, sheets and pillow cases and shirts follow suit down the line.

- Doesn't matter if the weather is sub zero...clothes will "freeze-dry." The wood stove will thaw a stiff pair of pants and shirt...and in the winter time, putting on warmed clothes is a regal treat.

- Always gather the clothes pins when taking down dry clothes! Pins left on the lines are "tacky!" Yes...maybe...well some of the time, not all of the time...forget the word 'tacky'...I always leave clothespins on the line, for those unexpected little jobs...like a towel or doggie bed that 'just has to be cleaned' a few pins are not a problem.

- If you really want to be efficient, line the clothes up so that each item does not need two clothes pins, but shares one of the clothes pins with the next washed item. I don't do this, although my

mom and grand-mom did...I like each item on its own, and sometimes with only one pin...if it's not too windy.

- Clothes off the line before dinner time, neatly folded in the clothes basket, and ready to be ironed.

IRONED? Just kidding...no ironing here. Not with the advent of 'wash and wear,' perma-pressed and even good old 100% cotton. It all dries great out in the sun and wind. I still have an ironing board and even a 'steam dry iron'...they are in the linen closet. I used to use the ironing board for sorting photographs and drying them.

But that's another story. For now, follow these handy rules for proper use of the clothesline. Satisfaction is bringing in clothers air-dried in sunshine. The aroma is intoxicating. This little story was totally inspired by Bob Dylan's 'Clothesline Saga'....a very funny tune...and very, very true to any of us who don't really mind doing laundry.

========= 30 =========

Isn't Life Beautiful

Years ago the famed Algonquin Hotel had its share of writers meeting around the table in New York. Designated a National Literary Landmark in 1996, in the early 1900s the establishment played host to daily meetings of journalists, authors, publicists and actors who gathered to share opinions and witticisms. A meeting of minds, as it were. Not to be outdone, the famed Chateau de Luna boasts an equal amount of talented writers and colorful characters as if channeling the muse of the famed Algonquin Round Table. Near the Rocks State Park, nestled amid the pines and Deer Creek, creative folks meet from time to time, mostly on the full of the moon. They have no agenda but to share in the camaraderie of tongues a-wagging so eloquently, there came a statement of note:

> "Word was delivered by messengers from the depths of Hell throughout the land of the infirm and obnoxious to gather upon righteous occasions to discuss and deliver words of wisdom to those less fortunate, the uninformed and unknown."

Lo and behold, such a birthing occurred less than 24 hours ago. The famed 'Chateau de Luna' boasts its own round table sort of. I received the invite and joined the proceedings. As is my custom for many affairs, 20 minutes in and I'd be ducking out the side door. Not this time. I joined the discussions and to my amazement,

spent the next four hours without time as my compass. At the end of the evening, the word was given. "And we were glad to have you." I'd be thrilled to add 'de Luna' as sacred grounds among the likes of Rustica and Environmental Evergreens. Our own personal, rotating version of H.S. Thompson's "Owl Farm" - where the best and brightest and weirdest gather to conspire, inspire, and howl at the moon.

So it is once again, folks of like mind and conscience are bound to find one another in this world of confusion, hate, apathy and distress. The Round Table of New York was one of those places and there are many others, both past and present. Doesn't have to be a classy hotel or a formal gathering hall either. The richness of these chance 'foundings' is often just the fact that we are in touch with someone else of a like mind. Sort of like how it used to be when we waltzed into Beakes' grocery or had a trim from 'Shorty' Garber. Today it might be the Super Thrift parking lot instead of Dick Rees' pool hall.

Or, chatting with others in the waiting room of Dr. Josiah Hunt's office on Main Street in Delta. You get the idea, or should by now. Folks just want to be friendly and share their thoughts, espouse an opinion, or just tell a story. It's our nature to do so. But in today's global yet isolated world of 'virtual this and that' and television and internet, we sometimes lose that blessing that we all shared at birth...the wanting of one another.

STH

When groups get together, it sometimes is a one man show, and we lose interest after a while. The true friends share equally, like we do in The Delta Crew...a remarkable union of adventurous brothers in and of itself. Now, here is another as yet unnamed combination of folks who are set upon to weave tradition with news and thoughts of the day. No lofty ideals, no agenda... just the gathering of kindred spirits.

ISN'T LIFE BEAUTIFUL?

Which leaves one to ponder, in the realest of senses... rescuing a beat up box turtle, lending a helping hand to an unwanted, large black snake from a friend's garden...it's all here for the asking. Called the 'Walden Experiment' we see friends and meet strangers with good intentions for the little time shared on this earth. We combine spirits to enhance, not break down...to preserve rather than exploit.

The work is hard, long and tiring as we get along in years...we see something every day and do our best to protect and defend the creatures who need our assistance. We feel good for what we've done if only to preserve something for a while longer.

Who knows when the last day will be, the day before we are no more and can do no more? Then, and only then, is when we trust in the great spirit to have influenced some other wandering soul to do the same and carry on...it's written and gathered in the stars.

========= 30 =========

Just Opening The Mailbag

C omes a time. I've been at this for quite a number of years folks and still enjoy telling tales and sharing stories and anecdotes of things I see and witness here and about. Of course, my main bread and butter for such a long time was photography...capturing the sights and recording life as it was and as it is. That's what I earned my living on for so long, whether holding a job at the local newspaper in Bel Air or running my own business. Still am as enthralled with the camera and what it can capture. But the days of being an ace cameraman have seen a different light of sorts and my scribbles mean as much to me as anything.

I've written about stepladders, statues of Mother Mary, snapshots of real folk in real-life situations, all with the hope that I've entertained, enlightened, and given something back to my friends and even readers who may never have heard of me. Never was about me so much as it was sharing my perspective on life so that others may enjoy and benefit from the ramblings of a participant in life.

In appreciation of the readers who write me notes, some need sharing and the sole purpose of this column is to acknowledge their thoughts, that others might feel the same about. Needless to say, when something hits home, at least for me, I want to share the feeling with whoever may be around at the time...thus, these notes that arrive

in my post office box are read and now shared with you. Enjoy them as I enjoyed receiving them.

The recent article about Koda's passing, prompted many readers of the Star to write, relating their own personal stories.

> Todd,
> I really enjoyed the article in the Star. About 11 months ago we had to put our dog Harley down, he was 12. So as I read your piece that flood of memories of my old buddy came pouring back to me. The time I had conversations with him on any number of topics, and he never so much as barked. Those memories will pop back into your head without prior notice when you least expect them, by something like your article. You did the old pooch justice. Tell your son to get another buddy soon, it will fill the fold of his old buddy. Remember my household is all women so I got out voted on the gender of the new puppy (as well as the name). But Rita has given us much new joy. (picture attached, the bow wasn't my idea either).
>
> Nice article, I enjoyed reading it.
> Take care,
> Jim H.

James M. Harkins
Director, Maryland Environmental Service

=========

Jefferey Wilson comments on the article about Sam Tharpe, retired Maryland State Trooper.

Dear Todd,

Thanks for the great article on Uncle Sam! He deserves it. The article was appreciated by the entire family. Uncle Sam has been flying on wings lifted by your article.
PAX!
JDW.

=========

This note from the Wiley family, of Delta, accompanied by a beautiful color photograph.

Hi Todd...Just finished reading your latest article in the Star...our favorite column each week..July 8th issue...really touched close to home for both of us.
Have had many pets over the years and as you said, they really become part of the family. And when they are gone it is heart breaking.
Enclosed is a favorite poem of mine. You may already have it, but when you read it (and I so believe it) it really touches your heart and I think just like your loved humans, you will also meet your beloved pets...
From Two fans of your articles, Joe and Nora Jane Wiley, Delta.

=========

The Wiley's enclosed a beautiful copy of Rainbow Bridge, a powerful farewell ode to a pet who's passed on. And no, I didn't have a copy of it...thank you!

Truly, the pups in my life, and Sam's, my son...all of us who've loved a pup or cat or bird...the loss of one is connected in some way to those other folks who share the same love affair with our 'silent pals'...who speak with tender eyes and kind attention whenever we walk in the door.

This has and will continue to be a recurring theme in my life and writing.

When you finish the Star today, it's summertime and hot, so put a bowl of ice cubes out for the pets.

========= 30 =========

The Times We've Known...

Sometimes when we're all alone we think of the times we've known, times of fun, sorrow, things long gone and hopefully, things to be...to become a memory in the future...dreams are what I'm talking about...they come often from the things we've known.

Times are changing as they always do...we can't lift the big stones we once placed so carefully along the wall around the flower beds...the canoe is a little harder to carry and put on the truck to go paddling. Subtly we are informed by our bodies that 'things aren't what they used to be.' The times we've known, and the times we live, today, now...are all threaded together like a large, random patchwork quilt.

Ran into a fella the other day, haven't seen him in over 35 years...just took different paths along the trail we all walk...and it was fine to see him. He remembered things I'd forgot and the same for him...but this time, I let the other guy do all the talking...usually I talk too much, but hey, I've got a lot to say, at least in my mind that's how I feel...it's like I've got to get it said or writ' before the curtain comes down.

Things I learned when the old bud and I were talking was that he is quite an accomplished guitar player and singer as well...he invited me up to Jack Kelly's to sit in and listen. Very modest, he continued that he's retired

from law enforcement and enjoyed the time spent with the badge and gun, but now he sings and plays guitar every chance he gets.

Mellow, easy with himself, it was a sign of what the times can be when you look back over the decades. We all are different now than we were then....change is inevitable and it can be for the good or the bad...what with sickness, death and folks being cut down long before their time.

Good pals are lost along the way, and others continue on...it's the luck of the draw I guess. Lots of things we forget, and then are reminded when we see an old friend from long ago...from high school, or our first job...or a family friend who just seems to last forever.

Today is a day like that...hard to tell what will come this way. Hopefully it's the same with you...running into someone from the long ago and far away. Hard to recognize some folks, and they look at us with that look in their eye that 'you've not missed many meals, eh Todd?'...and it's true...not the man I used to be in more ways than one....

In the ones that count though, the mind and memory are still in great shape and ready for more adventures and images and experiences. The times are tough right now...not as innocent as they used to be, and maybe that's a wake-up call that we have to get tough too... and that's a chore as we age and mellow, like my pal the

STH

former sheriff...we aren't of a mind to be 'tough'...we see and recall what things used to be like, how folks seemed to be a lot friendlier and of a kinder heart.

We can't change all that now, all we can do is be ourselves and be kind to one another and hope they return the favor. If they don't, well, we shake our heads and wonder why...and recall the best times of all... something the hard and fast will never know, not in the good sense we do.

========= 30 =========

Silver Star and a Touchdown or Two...

Wphen Sam Sheetz was wounded pulling fellow members of the infantry out of hostile fire in Vietnam he didn't think of the home runs he'd hit playing baseball as a youngster...or the touchdowns he scored playing halfback for Bel Air High School in the early 60s. All the thoughts of home runs or touchdowns were just as much a dream as the nightmare he was in right at that moment. As the battle raged all around him, there wasn't a moment to think of much of anything except the nightmare Sam was living.

He told me "some guys never get over it...the Vietnam thing...they never scored a touchdown, never hit a home run...all they did was survive a war like me and lots of others." There were lots more who didn't score the touchdown and didn't live to get the Silver Star, the Bronze Star or the Purple Heart...Sam did, but you'd never know it.

"This doesn't apply to the parents and families who lost a son or daughter in the war. For them the pain sometimes never goes away. When I speak of the war there are many aspects of unsung and 'overblown'... that's what I'm referring to...the ones who want to brag about heroics...the ones who never felt the 'rush'...I'm not interested in those stories," he notes as he elbow grease polishes a cherry drop-leaf table in his shop.

Sitting still is hard for Sam to do...just sitting is hard because of his combat wounds. Only you can tell how you would feel when someone who's been through the world of shit he has...speaks so blandly of it...to those who know, they do not speak...and often those who speak, do not know...the truth that is...truth and bravery have been instilled in Sam since early childhood and growing up in Harford County.

Sam came home and put his medals upstairs in his son's bedroom and no one ever sees them in the fine shadowbox his wife, Carolann, made for them. She is boldly proud of her husband of 42 years. A retired secretary from Havre de Grace High School, Carolann knows the values of hard work and perseverance. Twenty years ago Sam left his job with Whiteford Construction Company and started his dream, Grassy Creek Antiques & Country Store. Today it is a burgeoning business in Churchville occupying two buildings, several sheds, and an assortment of five huge trailers.

After his wife's retirement, they bought a place in Ocean City...where he sometimes takes time to 'get away.' But when home and on his 'regular' schedule, he just stays busy. Mondays, he repairs and restores antiques he searches for up and down the East coast. Sometimes on Tuesdays, he loads his truck and trailer with stuff that didn't make the 'cut' and sorts through the rubble. Wednesdays, he hauls out of his home in Aldino, Maryland, and by 5 a.m. is in Crumpton on the

STH

Eastern Shore. On the way home he may drop a line or two in Chester Creek, a rare break for a guy who never sits down and never dwells on heroics, let alone his own.

Thursdays, he is working again in his quaint shop behind his home. Fridays he has to pull 'shop duty' and is confined from 11 in the morning till the store closes at 5...then it's time for a Coor's Light and a few friends over for food he enjoys cooking on the grill.

The weekends are jam packed with antique auctions, sometimes two or three a Saturday...and the occasional Sunday 'public auction' at a rented hall.

Most Sundays he works more in the shop along Churchville Road, rearranging and answering questions from folks who expect to see him there. Today he's been asked to "find a spool bed, old and in good shape, cheap," he says with a smile.

"Yep, find it clean, not broke and cheap...right!" he adds.

Loading and unloading delicate antiques...bringing them to a sheen with rubbing and stroking...and it all begins again on Monday.

When a man loves his work it doesn't seem like work...and someone once said, "To do something you like and be paid to do it is the best of all situations to be in."

In all the years since that terrible war he rarely, if
ever, speaks of it and just plain never listens to others
speak of it. He shrugs at guys who hang around
the local 7-Eleven and boast of heroics while second
generation ears hang on every word. There are those
who lie about their heroics...men like Sam Sheetz are
likely to allow them short-shrift.

Dale Swanson, of Minnesota, a survivor from Sam's
Platoon, who readily admits he "owes his life to Sam"
contacted Carolann Sheetz and said a fellow comrade
was writing a book about Sam's courage under fire.

The book deals with the events of May 7-11 of 1968...
"when the LRRP (long range recon patrol) Team got
into real trouble on the ridge south of Camp Evans,"
according to potential author, Randy Kimes. "Your
(Sheetz's) platoon was RRF (rapid reaction force), and
inserted to 'assist' us getting out. Alpha Company was
inserted on May 9th to 'assist' your platoon."

Whatever the logistical confusion, the fighting was
intense and the realities of war were unforgiving...
only six out of the 40 men in Sergeant Sheetz's platoon
survived the ambush. The truth is the man in charge
of Sheetz's platoon 'froze' and Sam took over, calling in
artillery...and ended up saving Kimes' platoon as well.

Serving as squad leader with the second platoon of
Company B, 4th Battalion, 31st Infantry, 196th Infantry
Brigade, Sam Sheetz's squad was taken under fire and

quickly he laid down his own base of fire. He then had the wounded moved to the rear of the platoon while he moved forward to locate Kimes' LRRP Team.

Once that was done, Sheetz had three of his men evacuate the wounded, while he checked for more survivors. Next, he called in 'accurate artillery fire' for the remainder of the night.

"The morning after was foggy, not good, but our guys held and we got back down the mountain after a company relieved us...and they went right into the same mess we were in. I think the North Vietnamese Regulars were using the LLRP as bait to get our platoon. We were all over that country and within two weeks of getting there I knew with a map and compass exactly where I was, and it paid off calling in artillery accurately," Kimes relates.

While putting together the first draft of the book, Kimes contacted Swanson, looking for the man who had saved them. It was Swanson who vividly recalls the face of that football star from Aldino.

"Sam Sheetz is a hero and I wouldn't be alive today if it weren't for him," Swanson declares with honest and open appreciation. "His personal heroism and devotion to duty saved what was left after a horrific ambush."

Today, Sam Sheetz admits he never thought he'd speak to anyone who was on that hill ever again. A Silver Star was awarded Sheetz for that act of bravery and single mindedness, as well as a Bronze Star and Purple Heart.

His wife said the call was a voice from the past and it gave her man reason to pause...after he hung the phone up he uttered those words again...

"They never hit a home run...never scored a touchdown, all they have is the war and they need to get over it. There are a lot of guys who died there and their families will never 'get over it'...and there's nothing that can be done about that," Sam said.

From one who's been through a tough defense and firefights at night Sam Sheetz can say whatever is on his mind, without fear of contradiction. But mostly he doesn't say a word...he doesn't have to. Sam has had both battles...the gridiron and the battlefield. There were many who didn't have the luxury to play on the gridiron...and many who never got the chance to walk off the battlefield. That's something you just don't get over.

========= 30 =========

A Letter Written Long Ago

Funny how years ago, we wrote letters on an Olympia typewriter, or a Royal, or Smith-Corona...we wrote the letters, sometimes, not all the time made a copy for posterity and that was it.

Today we use the computer, save the message, file it with care and have instant access to it whenever the need arises. Technology can be a wonderful thing. Still, there was a sense of accomplishment and perhaps even a physical kind of thrill as the keys were pounded and the end of the line came and the ding signaled a carriage return was needed. Something about pulling that freshly written page out of the typewriter with something I had just written. The mind was actively engaged. The typewriter was tied to my thoughts.

My editor, Pat Wallis, has a lot of the 'hard copy' I've written over the years. He is always after me to do a book of the best stuff one day. I'm not sure anyone would want to read it, let alone buy a book of it...so it just sits in his library.

My son's birthday was September 12, and he turned 43. We spent the day splitting firewood here at Rustica for his wood stove. It was his choice, just to come out to the place, split as much wood as we could, share time with our pups and then grab a bite. It was a good call.

We got a lot done, had a grand time doing it. It was just the two of us, with of course, Roxy, Dude and Frisco. That's the way we celebrate a birthday. When Sammy left I did an e-mail check and had a note on the computer from Pat. Seems he had been going through some of my old stuff just to do a little organizing and had found something worth sharing. He knew it was Sam's birthday, but he didn't expect to come across what he did. Turns out it was a letter I had written long ago. I don't even recall writing it...nonetheless Pat felt it was fitting to send along. Pat, Sam, myself, and all who have since heard about this and have seen the letter agree it was both coincidental and a treasured find.

The A-Team at the game.

STH

Here is the letter in its entirety...I was thankful Pat had saved it. The words rang true then as they still do so today.

MAY 19ᵗʰ, 1988

Moving on to new adventures and new experiences I offer this simple prayer to my son, Sam.
May you sleep the sleep of rest and peace.
May your health continue to grow and be well.
May your days be filled with love and kindness,
and may those with you return with love and kindness.
May your trust in others be warranted.

May you reach others in need and may your needs be met.
Forget not your family, they have been with you, they know your way. Please let them be a part of your future as they have your past and present. As your days grow on be full with life and experiences.
Seek out the truth whenever you are in doubt.
It will never let you down.
Be cautious of new friends, let them earn your respect and they, yours.
Be not judgmental, rather insightful and open-minded.
There will always be other opinions, some right, some wrong, you will be the judge, and will live by your judgments.
Remember the days when you were a little guy, and the way you were, where your trails have crossed and how they have held you in good stead. You are what you are, the sum total of many people and many influences. Be proud of that, it was not in vain..
I can only write as a dad to a son, and the love is true and never was meant any other way, though your eyes and heart may have been hurt, the day will come when you will hurt with your eyes and voice too, and you will know the pain of one who casts the stone, as we all have done. It takes a man to acknowledge what he did that was wrong. First he must see the wrong and know he is responsible, those who hurt others and do not see what they have done are the lost. I've been lost and found more times than you have blown your nose, and I'm sure it will happen again. But remember, Sam, I've always been able to come back and make the slips less often.
I hope you can do that too
I hope we can always be best friends and stay in that special love of a son and a dad. My hope is to make our love last and flourish, something my dad and I ~~just couldn't~~ do, and no one there is to blame. I think it just makes me try harder to see around us and take the time to be free and honest and caring. I care, I love , I respect you, and in the end, that 's all there is, the rest is up to you.

Love and peace and understanding,
Your dad,. Your friend, Your co-conspirator

Whatever life lies ahead, we can be a part of all them, forever and ever.

========= 30 =========

Clear The Muddy Waters

This is a fast paced world we live in these days... days of confusion and doubt, fear and loathing. We search for little things that will offer a bright moment in our days. The ripple in the pond in the evening breeze. A call from an old friend to catch up on things. On a larger scale, however, there is little in the news that offers encouragement.

Was it after '9-11' that things were not as optimistic as before that clear and sunny September day? Waters got muddy after that indelible, tragic day. My son said later, *"Things will never be the same again, Dad."*

He was right...things change, we change, bad things happen to good people. No one wants to wash in muddy water...it's hard to see the good in muddy water...muddy water hides beauty and goodness.

What muddies the waters we live in? The media taking up causes that we know 'just aren't right'...trying to sway our thinking. The more we know of the truth, the more frustrated we become. Who can we trust with the information we are given in daily doses?

Muddy waters affect our co-workers, our friends and relatives, and our children. Only when we are strong enough to turn off the news, not be swayed...when we escape the mire, and talk one on one about simple truths...well, that's when we know there is something wrong elsewhere, out there, in the muddy waters.

Two of us, any of us, sitting around a table at home, maybe cruising about the county on a Sunday ride, discussing the life we live...it is then simple truths are revealed. It's refreshing to seek it, find it and share it...no matter what the subject...to simply relate facts without prejudice or muddy waters.

This is all well and good until we run into someone who has the proverbial 'axe to grind' or as I was once accused by a lady, 'an agenda'...hell, I'm the last person with an agenda...I don't know from one minute to the next what will come and go in my mind. All I know is truth, it's an easy thing for me to see and understand.

STH

Truth is fine with me, because I don't have the kind of memory it takes to come up with lies or agendas...truth be told, it's much easier to remember the truth...it's the lies in muddy water that are confusing to all of us...the tellers and the listeners.

I guess it's even tougher for those who work in office situations, big corporations or the government. I was lucky, self-employed with a creative job and life...art, photography and writing...it was so nice to just do what the work called for without concern for office politics or silly birthday parties every other day for the folk down the hall...whether we knew them or not. Or dodging the 'backstabbers' who only serve to disrupt the calmness of peaceful coexistence in the work place. From my unique vantage point, never really a part of working '9 to 5', I've listened to the stories my pals tell me...of the swayed opinions and mundane perspectives. Isn't that the workplace is bad, it's just a little murky to swim in.

I escaped muddy waters by being lucky enough to leave the corporate world of banking and set out on my own...how many of us wish we had taken that step into a life of uncertain but freewheeling work and earning a living? For all of those who for whatever reason weren't able to take that leap, I'll let you know that I honor and respect my vocation and try not to let anyone down.

A house of cards maybe, many have tried to leave the safe and secure paycheck to start a business only to have it fail through no fault of their own...so sure, it's a risky

business this act of leaving the guaranteed paycheck and waiting for the phone to ring for the work to come in... but that's just what keeps us out of the muddy water.

Each of us just does the best we can, hope for a little luck, and get on with our lives. Dad used to tell me when I was a kid on the farm and had no idea what I was gonna do when I grew up...

"Try to find something you like to do, that you're good at, and no one else is doing it...or there's not enough people doing it...it's a blessing to be paid to do something you love, Son."

I heard it, I get it, and I've repeated it to others.... Thanks, Dad.

========= 30 =========